Understanding
the Prophets

Understanding
the Prophets

BY SHELDON H. BLANK
Professor Emeritus
HUC-JIR

UNION OF AMERICAN HEBREW CONGREGATIONS
NEW YORK

Library of Congress
Catalogue Card No. 74-92159

First paperback edition 1983

© Copyright 1969
by
UNION OF AMERICAN HEBREW CONGREGATIONS
NEW YORK

Manufactured in the United States of America

Preface

In an earlier form this book was a course of lectures given before the Sixth Annual West Coast Teachers Institute (1965) at the UAHC Camp for Living Judaism, Saratoga, California.

It is not designed to teach a teacher how to teach the prophets. It is addressed to the teacher himself, or to any mature inquirer interested in knowing what the prophets can mean to a thoughtful man today. At best the book can teach him how to think about the Hebrew prophets.

An avid reader of Blank books will possibly discover in the following pages occasional (usually modified) quotations from *Prophetic Faith in Isaiah, Jeremiah: Man and Prophet*, and *The Dawn of Our Responsibility*. The translations from the Bible are my own.

I am grateful to JACK BEMPORAD, the Adult Education director of the Union of American Hebrew Congregations for encouraging me to publish this book and for his critical reading of the first typescript. I hope that I have made good use of his helpful suggestions.

S.H.B.

Contents

Understanding
the Prophets

The Harrowing Adventures
of Daniel the Jew

THE FIRST SIX CHAPTERS IN DANIEL'S BOOK COULD BE CALLED:
"The Harrowing Adventures of Daniel the Jew." What is
perhaps the best known tale among them, "Daniel in the
Lions' Den," is only one incident in his hazard-strewn career.
A starvation diet, a matching of wits with lives at stake, a
preheated fiery furnace, all figure along with the pit of lions
in Daniel's repertoire of horrors.

THE STORIES

Daniel is presented as one of four youths chosen from among
the exiled Judeans for an extended course of training at the
court of Nebuchadnezzar, king of Babylonia. Here, briefly
retold, is their first adventure:

Nebuchadnezzar charged his chief officer to include in his
academy certain captives from Israel—handsome, wise and
intelligent youths, one of them being Daniel. The king assigned them provisions from his own table and wine such as
he himself drank. For three years they were to be taught in
his school and fed on his food and then to be admitted to the
royal court.

3

Daniel and his friends accepted the stipends but they refused to touch the king's food. They would not soil themselves with it, they said; the chief officer should excuse them from that fare. But the principal was terrified. "I fear the king," he said. "Why should he find you scrawny among the well-fed students? You with your ritual diet! You put my head in jeopardy."

The most that Daniel could get as a concession was the chief officer's consent to a ten day test. Daniel and his friends would eat nothing but cereal with water for those ten days, and then the officer should see. So they did, and lo! at the end of ten days their faces were fairer and their flesh was fatter than all the youths who ate of the king's food. The chief had no need to fear, for God takes care of his faithful children.

So for the rest of their years at school they ate this simple food and studied hard and they graduated from Nebuchadnezzar's academy with a grade average ten times better than any on record. That last is a free translation. The usual translation reads: "In all matters of wisdom and understanding that the king inquired of them he found them ten times better than all the magicians and enchanters that were in all his realm." The king was obviously impressed.

The second adventure started with a dream. Nebuchadnezzar had a dream and he had to know what it meant. He ordered all of his magicians, astrologers, sorcerers, diviners and Chaldeans to interpret it for him—and just to make it harder he refused to tell them his dream. On pain of death they must both tell the dream and interpret it for the great king. Lamely they said if *he* would only tell *them* the dream they would surely tell him its interpretation. But the king was wise to their tricks, he said, and he told them to get on with the project if they did not want to be torn limb from limb and have their homes reduced to rubble.

It was then that Daniel came to the rescue, saving from that gory fate not only himself and his Jewish companions but all the wise men of Babylon as well. God listened to the prayer of the Jewish youths and revealed the secret to Daniel in a night vision. So Daniel blessed his God and went and told the king the dream along with its meaning. It was as simple as that. But to Nebuchadnezzar Daniel made it quite clear that not he but God had made the secret known. Again the mighty monarch was properly impressed.

The next adventure is the narrow escape from "the midst of the burning fiery furnace." Nebuchadnezzar made a golden image nearly a hundred feet in height, erected it in an open place, assembled his subjects and made proclamation: "Whenever you hear the music you must fall down and worship the image of gold that Nebuchadnezzar has made. And if you do not fall down when the music plays, that very hour you shall be cast into the midst of a burning fiery furnace." So all the king's subjects and all the king's men did as the king had commanded—all, that is, except, of course, the companions of Daniel. These youths refused and they said to the king: "If God whom we serve can save us He will save us even from the burning fiery furnace . . . but if not, be it known, O king, that *nevertheless* we will not serve your gods or worship the image which you have erected."

The angry king ordered the firemen to heat the furnace seven times hotter than ever before, to bundle the young men up in their robes, and to throw them into the roaring fire. Now, do not let anyone suppose that the fire was not *really* hot. It was so exceedingly hot that flames leapt out and destroyed the stout warriors who threw in the victims—*these* were burned to a crisp, but Daniel's friends walked about among the flames in cool disdain—the three of them along with an unidentified other presence who is later called an "angel." And a third time the king was greatly impressed.

Another dream and Daniel's correct interpretation—an interpretation which was *proved* correct by the fact that Nebuchadnezzar lived to experience what Daniel had fore-seen—led to no new dramatic experience, nor did Daniel's proper reading of the mysterious handwriting on the wall at

the feast of Belshazzar, a "son" or successor of Nebuchadnezzar; but each of these feats of wisdom too impressed a
king of Babylon.

Not only in Babylonia but also in the kingdom of Darius
the Mede this spectacular lad held a high office. Daniel's
success attracted the jealousy of political rivals there and they
conspired to destroy him, using his piety as a trap. This was
how they went about it: They persuaded Darius the king to
issue an edict, unchangeable, as were all the laws of the
Medes and the Persians. Whoever prayed for anything during the ensuing thirty days must direct his prayer not to God
but to the king—to Darius the king. If he prayed to any god
or man other than the king he would straightway be thrown
to the lions.

Now, though Daniel knew of the edict he went, *of course*,
as was his custom, to an upper chamber in his house and with
his windows open toward Jerusalem he knelt and prayed to
God three times a day. The conspirators, again *of course*,
promptly discovered his breach of the law and hurried off to
inform the king. Incidentally, this king Darius had grown
quite dependent on this Daniel and we have to pity him a
little. For not even he could change the law. Daniel was
thrown into the lion pit and the entrance closed with a stone.
Having then sealed it with his own signet to prevent any
trickery, the king dragged himself home to his palace, where
he passed the night fasting and with none of the usual royal
diversions. After a sleepless night he arose with the dawn and
ran straight to the lion pit. "O Daniel," he cried as he drew
near, "was your God whom you serve able to save you even
from the lions?"

We know the answer to the royal question, so we are
spared the pained suspense that held the king as he waited for
the seal to be broken and the stone rolled back. "O King, live
forever!" Daniel replied. "My God sent his angel [again, the
angel] and shut the lions' mouths. He found me innocent;

and also against you I have done no wrong." The king re-joiced.

Here again, let no one suppose that those lions were old and tame, well fed and toothless. When Darius had Daniel drawn up from the pit he ordered the conspirators fed to those same lions in Daniel's stead. In fact, for good measure he had their plump wives and their children thrown in too. And these choice morsels the lions caught in mid-air; indeed, before the victims reached the bottom of the pit, the lions had crushed *all* their bones. The lions were wild and hungry enough. And this king too—Darius the Mede—was mightily impressed.

These adventures all appear in the first six chapters of the biblical Book of Daniel. The stories are longer there, but they are the same stories. Those are the stories. Now, what do they mean?

THE SIGNIFICANCE

What are these tales? What shall we make of the adventures of Daniel the Jew and his Judean friends? If we say: "These things sound sort of miraculous," the obvious reply is this: "They sound that way because they are in fact sort of miraculous; and this indeed is the very point of Daniel's adventures: miracles happened to him." Miracles happened to Daniel in Babylonia as they happened for Aaron in Egypt, for Moses and Joshua at the Red Sea and the Jordan, as they did for Elijah and Elisha in Canaan—at least so the stories go. The miracles are meant to be: miracles.

The Daniel miracles are miraculous—and they convince these mighty kings, Nebuchadnezzar of Babylon, Belshazzar after him and Darius the Mede. The Daniel miracles were the reasons *they* gave—the reasons those kings gave for respecting Daniel's God.

In our review of these adventures of Daniel there is one point we have passed over too quickly, and it is this: the moral of the tales. As we consider them now again we seem to discern a pattern; they build up to a common conclusion: the miracles impress the kings; the kings are impressed and they must tell the world.

When Daniel interpreted Nebuchadnezzar's first dream, the great king "fell on his face" and worshipped him, the king worshipped Daniel and acknowledged Daniel's God. Then the king declared: "In very truth your God is the God of gods, the Lord of kings who reveals the secrets of the future, as He has done through you . . ." Yes, "the God of gods, the Lord of kings" (2:47).

Nebuchadnezzar's second dream, Daniel's explanation, and the dream's fulfillment, led the king again to say: "I, Nebuchadnezzar, praise and extol and honor the King of the heavens, for all His works are truth, His ways are justice, and He is able to humble those that walk in pride" (4:34). Let it be understood: This is no Hebrew prophet speaking here—no king of Israel, no priest or psalmist. This is a king of Babylon.

When Daniel's companions came from the burning fiery furnace unsinged, Nebuchadnezzar blessed the God that sent His angel and saved His trusting servants even from the king's command, and he issued this decree: that any people, nation or language that speaks anything amiss against this God should be torn limb from limb and their homes be reduced to rubble, because, he said, there *is* no other god that can save in such manner (3:29).

The second royal edict introducing the narration of the king's second dream was less edict than testimonial. It reads:

> Nebuchadnezzar the king, to all the peoples, nations, and languages that dwell in the whole earth, great be your peace! It has seemed good to me to make known the portents and wonders that God Most High has per-

> formed. . . . His kingdom is an everlasting
> kingdom and His dominion is from generation
> to generation (3:31–33).

And finally, when Daniel came up, with not a single scratch, from the lion pit, Darius the Mede made proclamation that in all the dominion of his kingdom men must tremble and fear before Daniel's God: for "He is the living God," he said, "and His kingdom shall never be destroyed. He who saved Daniel from the jaws of the lions saves and delivers, performs portents and works wonders in the heavens and on the earth" (6:27f.). Not just in Persia or in Babylon—notice: "in the heavens and on the earth."

That, indeed, is the point of all these narratives. Those lords of the empires between the two rivers, kings of Babylon and a king of Persia, were convinced. Because of the miracles, because God, the God of Daniel and his companions, had revealed the secrets of the future, had miraculously intervened to save His servants from starvation, had delivered them from death in the burning fiery furnace, had saved them from death in the lion pit, those ancient mighty kings were convinced, said the author of the Book, that God is God. These reasons were good enough for them. Those monarchs were ready; after they had seen what they had seen and heard what they had heard they were ready to issue decrees and publish abroad the wondrous news; they were the witnesses and they sent out their heralds to spread the new gospel—royal missionaries, missionary kings from Babylonia and Media, foreign witnesses to Daniel's God.

THE AUTHORS AND THEIR MESSAGE

The biblical authors who told these stories enjoyed the telling; they found pleasure in the record. They were proud of the supposed fact that men of the stature of a Nebuchadnezzar and a Darius spoke with such undisguised enthusiasm about the God of Israel. To each other the Jews had said: Hear, O Israel, the Lord our God alone is God. For generations they had said it. It was another thing to hear it now proclaimed by the rulers of the great empires of the nations, the Gentiles. That was a great satisfaction. Entertaining though these stories are, whoever told them obviously meant to do more than simply entertain his hearers. They are fiction certainly, but fiction with a purpose, and a message. What message comes through depends on the hearer. If he is a servant of Daniel's God, this is one of the things that the stories say to him: Be proud of your heritage. See how God's majesty excited royal strangers and cherish the privilege you enjoy as His servant. If he who hears or reads the stories is not a worshipper of Daniel's God they speak to him of the eminent advantages which men enjoy in the fellowship of such a God.

The stories never suggest that those kings in Daniel or their people became proselytes, like Ruth taking "refuge under the wings of the Lord, the God of Israel"—that does not seem to be the writer's concern; but the stories do say that those kings recognized Israel's God as God. This they say repeatedly and emphatically, as though to make a point of it. The moral is there for all to read. The author of the Daniel narratives had the unabashed spirit of a missionary. He was proud of his heritage, and he generously wished all men to share his exuberant faith in the greatness and goodness of his God. He was not writing "literature." This dedicated man was writing with a high and serious purpose.

In this respect, of course, he was not different from the other men whose collected words we call the Bible. The Bible is a great literature, but the men who made it did not at all set out to create literature. They spoke with a holy purpose. The discovery of that purpose is both a goal and a reward of Bible study. The Daniel stories serve as an illustration of this first observation: that the men who created the books of the Bible were moved by a sacred purpose.

THE BOOK OF DANIEL

It may seem strange to some that we approach our study of the prophets and prophetic thought by way of Daniel. We may appear to be starting at the end rather than the beginning of our subject. For, according to the order of the biblical books in the Hebrew Scriptures, the Book of Daniel comes near the end of the canon, and also, according to a large consensus of scholars, the Book of Daniel was composed at or near the end of the biblical period.

One might even question the propriety of calling Daniel a prophet. We will find the Book of Daniel among the prophets, or fail to find it there, depending on what text we are using. In the early Greek translation (the Septuagint) this Daniel book is one of the books of "the Prophets." Not so in the Hebrew Scriptures; there it appears among the "Writings" or Hagiographa. Some English translations follow the order of books in the Septuagint, others the Hebrew order. In the standard translation of the Jewish Publication Society, for example, Daniel comes just before Ezra, Nehemiah and Chronicles, among the last of the books in the Hebrew Bible.

Most modern language translations follow the Septuagintal order, with Daniel as a sort of appendix to Ezekiel. How it got there is easy to see: the Babylonian king whom Daniel mentions, Nebuchadnezzar, belongs to the time of Ezekiel. But this clue is misleading and most scholars correctly assign the Book of Daniel to a later century. As with much historical fiction the time of the author is remote from the time of the characters; though indeed the scene is laid in the Babylonian period the book was in fact composed centuries later. As we have it the book belongs to the Maccabean age at the close of the biblical period. The clues for this dating appear mostly in the second half of Daniel, in the six other chapters which we have not even mentioned, and they point uniformly to the second pre-Christian century and the time of the cruel Antiochus. So the book was written too late to find a place among the Prophets and, according to the grouping of books in the Hebrew Scriptures, it appears instead among the Writings.

Nevertheless there are reasons for associating this little book with the prophetic literature as we have done here, and one of these reasons is the presence of those miracle tales in the first six chapters of Daniel. This is the feature of the book which makes it a good starting point for an exploration of prophetic thought. The harrowing adventures and the repeated miraculous deliverance of Daniel and his three friends are very like those related in the "Former Prophets," mainly in the books of Samuel and Kings, and notably associated there with the persons of Elijah and Elisha. The neatly patterned and manifestly motivated miracle tales in Daniel open the way for us to an understanding of comparable tales in Samuel and Kings. What motivated the author of these moved also the authors of those, and our excursion into the first half of the Book of Daniel has been an introduction to the stories of miracles told of Elijah, Elisha, and even Isaiah.

But before we go on to those earlier tales, we make one further observation about Daniel. View the book as a product of a time of religious persecution and the stories become significant in yet another way. They carry this weighty message: that even when circumstances are wholly desperate the faithful can rely on the help of God. If only a miracle can deliver his people God will perform that miracle; they need not fear. Against discouragement in grim and bitter times, God seems to be saying to His people: "Be still and know that I am God, exalted among the nations, exalted on the earth" (Ps. 46:11).

The Meaning behind the Miracle

Using as a background this look at the first half of the Book of Daniel, we can turn to the similar tales in Samuel and Kings and, so prepared, read them with a measure of new understanding.

A STORY ABOUT THE STORIES

Start with a story about the stories. It is found in the Second Book of Kings and it too throws light on the nature of these tales and especially on the manner in which they were preserved. Here in Second Kings reference is made to Elisha's wondrous feat in Shunem, where he restored to life the son of his wealthy benefactress. His deed is related in the fourth chapter of the book but here at the beginning of the eighth we have a dramatic allusion to that earlier miracle.

Now Elisha had said to the woman whose son he had revived:

> "Get up and go, you and your family to live somewhere else, because God has announced a famine here which will last seven years." So the woman did as the man of God had urged. She and her family went and lived for seven years in Philistia. Then after seven years she returned from Philistia and set out to lay

her claim before the king for home and field.
The king just happened to be talking with
Gehazi, the disciple of that man of God:
"Tell me," said the king, "all the wonders
which Elisha wrought." And Gehazi was just
telling the king that [Elisha] had revived the
dead child, when the woman whose son he
had restored to life laid her claim for home
and field before the king. So Gehazi said:
"My lord, O King, here is the woman and
here is her son." Then the king asked the
woman and she told him; and the king had
her property returned to her together with
all that her field had produced in her absence
(II Kings 8: 1–6).

Readers may notice one feature or another as they read this
account, but one who is interested in the literary history of
the Bible will certainly notice first of all the opening words
of the king to the prophet's disciple: "Tell me all the
wonders which Elisha wrought." This is the king speaking;
tired of "counting out his money," the king takes this time
off to ask the young man to tell him a story. He has certainly
heard this story before, since he knows that Elisha has done
noteworthy deeds—*gedolot*, he calls them, "great deeds"—
but he wants to hear it again. It is a good story and he finds it
both entertaining and edifying.

No doubt it is by some such process that these stories came
to be. They were told, we may suppose, from mouth to
mouth; the king does not read this story from a scroll—he
asks to be told. No doubt too the tales grew in the telling.
They were cherished, treasured, some of them chuckled
over, some marvelled at—and in course of time collected,
recorded, organized, and eventually incorporated into our
Book of Books.

It is fortunate for us that these stories were thus admired.
Without them we should probably know little if anything
about the so-called Former Prophets, Samuel, Nathan, Gad,

Elijah, Elisha, Micaiah and their company. That, of course, is a major difference between the "Former Prophets" and the "Latter Prophets"—their literary history. We know about the former because of the stories men told—what those prophets said is not on record, or it appears only as a terse punch line in a tale. About the latter, beginning with Amos, some stories indeed are told but we know these prophets best as men of words. What they themselves *said* far outweighs what others related as tales and legends to edify and to entertain. That is why we often call these latter prophets "the literary prophets"; because what we see when we look at the books named after them is what they said, and not the stories told about them. But our present interest is in the stories told in the Former Prophets.

THE MIRACLE TALES IN THE FORMER PROPHETS
AND WHAT THEY PROVE

A sacred purpose moved the men who wrote the narratives in Samuel and Kings even as it did the authors of the Daniel stories. Think now first of what was told about Elijah and the poverty-stricken woman of Zarephath. There is no humor here. Here is stark need and terror. The story is told in the seventeenth chapter of First Kings. A woman and a land were widowed. The land bore no crops of grain and oil because there was no rain. The woman and her son had reached the end of their resources. When Elijah found the woman outside the wall and said to her: "Fetch me a little water in a bowl to drink," and again: "Bring also a bit of bread," she had to say: "As the Lord your God lives, I have no store at home, only a handful of flour and a small flask of oil. I was just finding a couple of sticks to go in and prepare [bread] for myself and my son; then we would eat it—and die."

You remember the miracle then, and its terrifying sequel—one on the heels of the other—how first, when she had shared their little with the prophet, wondrously the remainder was replenished, repeatedly replenished until the rains came, and how, after that, the boy grew ill and died and Elijah restored him to life—as later Elisha was to do under similar circumstances for another lad.

Now observe one of the significant details in this story. It concerns the "*word* of the Lord." When the widow told Elijah what she was about to do he ordered her to provide for him first and then for herself and her son out of the pitiful remainder—but not to die. "Because," he said, "so the Lord God of Israel has said: The sack of flour will not be exhausted and the flask of oil will not be emptied before God gives the soil its rain." And this part of the story concludes: "The sack of flour was [in fact] not exhausted and the flask of oil was not emptied, in full accord with the word of the Lord which He spoke through Elijah." N.B.! "the word of the Lord which He spoke through Elijah." This is the theme which the narrator picks up as his punch line again at the end of this whole story.

After Elijah has given life back to the boy and has said to the mother: "See, your son is alive," then the woman is convinced. She says to Elijah: "Now in truth I know that you are the man of God and that the word of the Lord is in your mouth"—again "the word of the Lord"! This climactic sentence reveals the narrator's purpose. It tells what the story is about. Aside from its primary purpose, power to buttress the faith of the needy, it served to authenticate God's prophet. "The man of God" could be recognized by his wondrous deeds. These were his credentials and such a man must be believed. When he claims to speak "the word of the Lord" we must believe him.

This is not unique—this illustration of the thought that miracles served in biblical times to authenticate the prophet. Remember Elisha's word to the king of Israel. Elisha's king was in a panic because the mighty king of Syria had sent to him his general to be cured of his disease. Elisha heard of it and sent a message to the king. "Why are you tearing your hair out, your majesty? Let this fellow come to me and he will learn that there is a prophet in Israel" (II Kings 5:8). The first part of this message is a free translation but the end is not: he will learn (from the miraculous cure) what? That Elisha is a prophet. The cure will authenticate the prophet—it will do something else as well, but this in the first place.

The chapters in Exodus that tell of Moses and Aaron at the court of Pharaoh and what we usually call "the ten plagues"—those four or five chapters have a complicated literary history, but one of the several versions of those incidents there belongs in this context. Pharaoh wants evidence that Moses and Aaron are what they claim to be. "Produce your credentials," he demands (Exod. 7:9) or, as in the new JPS *Torah*, "Produce your marvel" or, as in *Green Pastures*, "Pass a miracle." Whatever criteria we might ask today, only miracles would convince Pharaoh then that Moses and Aaron spoke for the Lord.

This kind of thinking occurs again in Ezekiel (*e.g.* 12:27f.), in the Second Isaiah (*e.g.* 44:25f.), and in Zechariah (*e.g.* 2:13,15), and it may have originated at the time of the Babylonian Exile, when so many other things were happening to the religion of Israel.

Pause here: For the writers of the Bible the performance of miracles passed as evidence that a man was a prophet. These may not be our criteria, but among the reasons those men gave for believing that a prophet truly spoke the word of the Lord was his ability to make accurate predictions and to do other such miraculous things.

THE LORD IS GOD

But the predictions and the other miracles seemed also to prove something else. As in the Daniel stories they proved that "the Lord, He is God."

Consider in this connection the story of Elijah at Mt. Carmel—or not the whole already familiar story, but one detail early in the narrative—and then the punch line at the end. The earlier detail is a part of Elijah's proposal. After describing the whole arrangement for the contest between himself on one side and the 450 Baal prophets on the other— with the altars and sacrifices fuelled and prepared, he proposed in conclusion: "Then you shall call on the name of your god and I on the name of Israel's God and it is understood that the god who responds with fire, he is God." Then all the people consented: "It is understood" (I Kings 18:24). The narrator goes on to tell of the contest—the wildly orgiastic prophets of Baal, their dancing and shouting, and their failure; the methodical preparations of the lone Elijah, his prayer, and his success. Finally then the meaning of it all: "The whole people saw, fell down in worship and said: The Lord alone is God! The Lord alone is God!" That is the issue and the consummation.

Naaman's story, as we have seen, authenticates Elisha, but it does something else as well, and in doing so it goes beyond the story of Elijah at Mt. Carmel too. Naaman, not a Hebrew but a Syrian general, a soldier in the army of a foe of Israel, learns through the miracle of his recovery from disease that Elisha who sent him to bathe in the Jordan is a *nabi*, a prophet, but the climax in his story comes when he speaks very much the same as Nebuchadnezzar and Darius spoke in the Daniel stories. "He returned to the man of God, he and all his camp, and he entered and stood before him and said: so, now I know that there is no god in all the earth except in Israel. . . ." And he added: "Henceforth your servant will offer no sacrifice or offering to any god other than the Lord" (II Kings 5:15-17). From the event Naaman concludes that Elisha is an authentic prophet of Israel's God but, even more significantly, he concludes that Israel's God alone is God, and he even goes on to the practical consequence: Henceforth this enemy of Israel will worship Israel's God and worship none other. A missionary spirit motivated the writer of this Naaman story, even as in a later century it moved the author of the miracle tales in the Book of Daniel.

There is also something in the Exodus stories that we can understand a little better after this review. It is that puzzling bit about God's hardening Pharaoh's heart. It is a theologically embarrassing business—God's making the king stubborn and then punishing him for it; punishing him for what he could not help, for what was not even his own doing. The business becomes somewhat less puzzling and slightly less embarrassing theologically when we recognize that the hardening of Pharaoh's heart belongs to the same version of the Exodus story as the miracles. Like Naaman, the Syrian soldier, Pharaoh, the king of Egypt, learned more than that Moses and Aaron were authentic spokesmen for their God. Pharaoh learned also that their God is God, superior indeed to the presumed gods of his vast realm, superior even to the divine Pharaoh himself. God could, of course, have omitted the demonstration, could simply have led His people out of Egypt. But that would not so well have served God's broader purpose. "This is why I prolonged the affair," God says to Pharaoh, "to show you My strength, to make My name known in the whole earth" (Exod. 9:16).

In the end God did of course let fall upon Pharaoh climactic disaster to teach him, as God said, "that there is none like Me on earth" (9:14). God did not so much harden Pharaoh's heart as make him skeptical so that he would withhold belief until the demonstration was concluded. When the wise men and magicians of all Egypt lost the contest—when the snake that was Aaron's rod devoured the snake that was their magic-working staff, when they could not, like Aaron, turn dust into lice and informed the Pharaoh confidentially: "This is the finger of God," when far from making the soot of a furnace produce sore boils on others they themselves were so sorely afflicted that they could not even stand before Moses, Pharaoh still demurred. It was the death of Pharaoh's son together with all the other first-born sons of Egypt that effectively erased his doubt.

This does not make a nice story. It was not nice either when Darius threw to the lions the wives and children of the conspirators in the Daniel story. Recall the cruelty of the Egyptian taskmasters, the plotting of the Persian conspirators, the cruelty of Antiochus, and charge these excesses to the account of poetic justice. Then focus rather on the purpose of the biblical authors who wanted all the world to know the greatness of their God—to share their knowledge of God, first, no doubt, with their own people, but then as well with all the nations of the world.

THE REASONS MEN GIVE

Finally this observation: While we may applaud the purpose of the dedicated men who wrote the miracle tales—in Daniel and Kings and elsewhere in the Bible—we surely bring more enthusiasm to their purpose than to their reasoning. But this is not serious, because the reasons men give are often a matter of fashion or style. A truth may be truer than the reasons we give to support it. And a truth may remain a truth long after the reasons we give have gone out of fashion.

This last observation is not meant as a suggestion that we should simply believe, take things "on faith," rely on authority. On the contrary, we may well suspect those things that we simply believe—without reason. We *should* examine our beliefs and find out for ourselves whether they are true or false. They could be superstitions; they could be prejudices—or propaganda—they could even be malicious lies.

Reasons, indeed, have their fashions. What convinced Pharaoh that the God of Aaron was God? The fact that Pharaoh's court magicians were not able to copy all of the miracles that Aaron performed, the fact that Aaron could "pass" a better miracle through the power of his God than they with the aid of the gods of Egypt. What convinced the prophets of Baal that Elijah's God was God? The fact that Elijah defeated the prophets of Baal in the test at Mt. Carmel; it was Elijah's God, not Baal, that sent the fire from heaven which licked up the barrels of water and consumed the sacrificial bull on the altar. What convinced the Syrian captain Naaman that Elisha's God was God? The fact that Elisha cured this captain's ailment with Jordan water. What reasons did Nebuchadnezzar advance, and Darius, when they testified that Daniel's God was the God of gods and the Lord of kings, the living God whose kingdom shall never be destroyed? The fact that He revealed the secrets of the future, sent His angel and delivered His trusting servants from the burning fiery furnace, saved Daniel from the jaws of the lions, performs wonders and works miracles in heaven and on the earth. For what are Jews traditionally grateful when year after year they light the lights of Chanukah and praise the Lord? That it was He "who wrought wonders for our fathers at that season in those days."

Look back now at those stories of Daniel and the others and ask the right question. Do not ask: What really happened? To say that "Daniel was a dentist and he pulled the lions' teeth" is to miss the point of the story completely. The point of the story is that a miracle occurred. The story is not a record of an event; it is the tale of a miracle. Do not ask: What really happened? Do not even ask: What does this miracle mean to me? It means nothing; it is a good story but "it ain't necessarily so." Ask the right question. Ask: What did these miracles mean to the dedicated authors of the book of the adventures of Daniel the Jew and of the other books of miracle tales? The answer to that question should now be clear. Miracles were the reasons that those men gave. They were the reasons men gave in those days, the credentials of God, the proofs men needed then, arguments that convinced a Pharaoh, the worshippers of Baal, a Naaman, a Darius, and a Nebuchadnezzar. Miracles were in fashion then. For the most part they have gone out of fashion today. We do not put much store by miracles; we simply try to understand the stories in their setting. If today we say: The Lord our God alone is God, we say it with no recourse to miracles as reasons. If miracles were to do anything to our belief today they would probably add not to our faith but to our doubts about the stability of our world.

We have come a long way from the lion pit. The reasons that seemed convincing to the tellers of tales about Daniel and Elisha are no longer the reasons we give. In the wondrous structure of subatomic matter and of the countless solar systems, in their very orderliness and consistency, in the unlimited capacity of men to love each other as one vast brotherhood, in these we see the surest signs that one spirit moves in all.

Our reasons are different but our conclusions and our envisioned goals agree with those of the tellers of miracle tales. The truth which they meant to proclaim is the truth which still we teach to one another when we say: "Hear, O Israel," the truth which we teach to the peoples of the earth when we are faithful to our mission: that the Lord indeed is God. And the goal which they set for themselves is the goal of which we still speak today: a reconciled humanity, peace on earth and freedom.

On beyond Stories

THREE KINDS OF REPORTS

CONSIDER THREE SEPARATE VERSES FROM THE BOOK OF AMOS
and decide who the speaker is in each.

Here is the first of the three:

> Amaziah, the priest of Beth-El, sent word to
> Jeroboam, the king of Israel, saying: Amos
> has conspired against you in the midst of
> Israel; the land cannot contain all his words
> (7:10).

Who is the speaker? Not Amaziah, not Jeroboam, not Amos,
but an unnamed other person. A narrator, a reporter, a
biographer, unnamed, is speaking about Amaziah the priest,
about Jeroboam the king and about Amos the prophet. This
verse is a part of a third person narrative about Amos, similar,
in form at least, to the stories about prophets considered
above—the stories about Elijah and Elisha, about Moses and
Daniel. The form is the same, but there is a difference which
we will yet observe.

The second example:

> Thus God the Lord showed me and lo! a
> basket of ripe summer fruit; and He asked:
> What do you see, Amos? And I said: A
> basket of ripe summer fruit . . . (8:1f.).

Who? Yes, Amos is speaking. He is his own narrator here, relating his own experience. He is speaking autobiographically, giving first person testimony, getting it into the record. This form is new to our study, but we shall have more of it. It sounds as if it might be the most reliable of all forms, the least subject to change through misunderstanding or misinterpretation.

Now the third example:

> Did you bring Me sacrifices and offerings
> those forty years in the wilderness, O house
> of Israel? (5:25)

Who? Yes, now it is God speaking. The first person pronoun "Me" stands for God. He is addressing the people of Israel and He expects them to agree with the implications of His rhetorical question, to admit that they did not bring Him sacrifices those forty years in the wilderness. One might object when we say that God is speaking here, and we would have to agree that the reporter is, in fact, the prophet. It is God's word through Amos—not heard by us directly but only as reported by the prophet—and we accept it as God's word or refuse to do so, depending on whether we are willing to believe that Amos heard and truly reported the word of God.

The three forms of prophetic tradition are before us: (1) stories about a prophet told by a biographer, i.e., by a narrator other than the prophet himself; (2) stories about a prophet told by the prophet himself in the first person or autobiographical form, and (3) words spoken by God through the prophet.

Our interest will eventually center on the third of these forms, the prophetic word attributed by the prophet to God. But first we want to note a few more things about the first of these forms and quite a bit more about the second form.

THE BIOGRAPHICAL FORM

First then, the biographical form. How good are the stories about the prophets? If "good" means "historical" they are of varying quality. Some are simply fiction—not historical at all. But there are values other than historicity, as we shall yet note.

Though for the most part stories about prophets occur in the books of Samuel and Kings, we find them too in Isaiah, Jeremiah, Ezekiel and the Twelve. We turn now to these—to the biographical parts of these latter books, the books of the prophets known as the Latter Prophets.

Some of the biographical passages there throw proper light on the lives of some prophets. Some are more reliable than prophet stories in Samuel and Kings—and certainly more so than those in Daniel. We know more about Amos, having the story in his seventh chapter, than we would know without that narrative. We know much more about Jeremiah, having the biographical chapters which appear in his book, than we would know without those chapters. Nearly all that we know about Haggai we derive from the plausible third person narrative which makes up his book.

But not all the biographical material is equally reliable. In the books of Hosea and Isaiah the matter is complicated. The first chapter of Hosea tells the story of his married life in biographical form. In his third chapter Hosea may be telling the same story himself now in the first person or auto-biographical form. We would have a clearer picture if instead of the two we had only the one or the other of these parallel narratives.

Isaiah's biographer has done real mischief. He gives us a picture quite different from the one we can reconstruct from Isaiah's few first person narratives and from the words of

God as reported by this prophet. The one or the other is unhistorical. An examination of the biographical chapters makes it pretty clear which form of narrative, the biographical or the autobiographical, is the more reliable. The better narrative is the one told in the first person form.

What impression does one get, for example, from a narrative like the following, excerpted from the thirty-eighth chapter of Isaiah?

> And the word of the Lord came to Isaiah saying: Go, say to Hezekiah, So said the Lord the God of your father David: I have heard your prayer, I have seen your tear; I will add to your life fifteen years; I will deliver you and this city from the king of Assyria's hand; yes, I will shield the city. And this shall be your sign from God the Lord that the Lord will do as He has said: the shadow on the dial which has advanced on the sundial of Ahaz I will set back ten degrees. Thereupon the shadow which had advanced on the dial did turn back ten degrees. [And then the continuation a bit further on] So Isaiah said: Let them take a cake of figs and rub it on the abscess and he will be cured (38:4–8, 21).

When one hears this story one thinks of the miracle tales told in the books of Samuel and Kings—of the "man of God" splitting the altar at Beth-El, or Elijah calling down fire from heaven, or Elijah dividing the Jordan, or Elisha defying the force of gravity and causing an ax-head to float. In that same fashion here Isaiah turns the shadow back on the sundial, ten degrees. One thinks also of Nathan accepting King David's penitence and lifting the death sentence, or Elijah approving Ahab's act of self-mortification and sparing him. In that same fashion here, when Hezekiah on his sickbed, hearing that he is to die, prays and weeps, Isaiah adjourns the evil day for fifteen years. So too one remembers Elisha's extracting the poison from a brew with nothing but flour, and curing Naaman's ailment with only Jordan water. In that same way Isaiah here heals King Hezekiah's seemingly mortal illness, using only a simple home remedy—a poultice of figs. Although it now appears in the Book of Isaiah, the narrative has the features of a miracle tale. Is this book its original home?

RELIABLE HISTORY?

The story just quoted is one of the "duplicate" texts in the Bible. There are a number of such texts. Large blocks of material in Samuel and Kings appear again in Chronicles. The "swords into plowshares" passage appears in Micah 4 as well as in Isaiah 2. And Psalm 18 is to be found not only between Psalm 17 and Psalm 19 but in the twenty-second chapter of Second Samuel as well. So too this story of Hezekiah's encounter with the prophet Isaiah; we find it in the thirty-eighth chapter of Isaiah, but we also find it in the Book of Kings. Most of chapters 36 to 39 of Isaiah duplicate most of chapters 18 to 20 in Second Kings.

To say they are duplicates is a cautious way of speaking. Throwing caution to the winds we ought simply to say these chapters in Isaiah are more properly at home in the Book of Kings, from which place someone copied them out, making only minor changes, to serve as a supplement or appendix to the Book of Isaiah. One of the facts which suggest this conclusion is their position in the book. Before "the Second Isaiah" was added to the first (Chapters 40–55 of Isaiah to Chapters 1–39) these chapters (36–39) stood just where we would expect to find an appendix—at the end of the book of that first Isaiah.

Speculate with me a while. Let us make two "supposes" and follow them with two observations. Suppose, in the first place, that we had no book of Isaiah. Would we know anything about the prophet Isaiah? Yes, of course, we would know what we read of him in those chapters 18–20 in Second Kings. But what kind of a picture would that material yield? The Isaiah we would know with only Second Kings to draw on would be an Isaiah far different from the one our more credible other sources yield. The popular image of the prophet in Kings is qualitatively different from the one which our more credible other sources yield. The popular image of the prophet in Kings is qualitatively different from the real Isaiah; wholly absent from the popular image are those features of his life and thought, which alone distinguish him and which alone make of him a towering figure in the history of the human spirit and the growth of conscience. Fortunately for Isaiah and for us, we have more than the distorted record of his life and thought which his biographer bequeathed to us in Second Kings and this appendix to Isaiah's book. A prophet concerned for his personal immortality should find a more reliable biographer—or he should be a literary prophet, i.e., he should himself report his life story and take pains himself to record his utterances.

Now let us leave Isaiah and make a second "suppose." Reverse the process and now suppose that, in addition to the story told of the little known prophet Ahijah of Shiloh in 1 Kings 14:1–18—suppose we had a book of Ahijah even as we have a book of Isaiah (it would not have to be sixty-six chapters long; it could also be a little book like the nine chapters of Amos), what then would we be able to say of Ahijah? Or substitute for Ahijah in this speculative question the name of Nathan or Gad, Elijah or Elisha, Micaiah or Huldah the prophetess, any of the prophets whom we know now from the Book of Kings only—what greatness might we not find in any of them if we had their own stories and their own record of the words of God which they spoke?

So now the first observation: For our knowledge of the *lives* of most biblical prophets we depend on stories which were told about them by others and these stories are, for the most part, piteously inadequate. And yet, for a few of the Latter Prophets (Amos, Jeremiah and Haggai, for example) some of this biographical material is significant and most welcome. We would be hard put to reconstruct the histories of these few if their biographers had not left even these sparse records.

WHAT THE BIOGRAPHIES DO SAY

This, now, is the second observation about the biographical material in the prophets: Fiction often says things that histories overlook, or, stated differently, the stories about the prophets are a valuable source for information other than that concerned with the lives of those prophets. We have been speaking with little enthusiasm about the prophet stories or biographical matter in Isaiah and in Samuel and Kings, and in Daniel, as a source for the life stories of prophets. If through the camouflage of fiction prophets like Elijah and Elisha and others become visible at all, they emerge romanticized and barely credible. But there is another side to the coin: as we have already noted, this same fiction says much about the *tellers* of these stories and about the society in which they grew. From their miracle tales those writers look out as men with a mission, men concerned to spread knowledge of Israel's God among the peoples and across the broad earth—concerned also, perhaps secondarily, to establish the authority of prophetic voices in their own society.

Interesting people, these authors and their society, as they are revealed in the prophet stories they tell! These authors and this people cherished the tradition that their prophets, speaking for their God, held their kings in check, that the kings of Israel and Judah govern with God's consent and rule only so long as they accept God's way. With few exceptions, according to these authors, every king in all the long history of the two kingdoms, had a prophet at his side to approve his actions or rebuke him as his conduct merited. These writers assume that at God's bidding prophets made kings and deposed kings, advised kings on matters military and religious, admonished kings and directed them in ways of morality, justice and faithfulness. They understood their form of government to be a "limited" monarchy, their monarchs limited by the voice of their God sounded by His prophets.

Another thought of theirs, a related thought, is this: that history does not simply happen. Throughout the period of the kingdoms, according to the authors of the books of Samuel and Kings, whenever and wherever history is being made a prophet is on the scene to interpret the event and to show where it fits into the pattern of history divinely ordained.

Those are some of the thoughts which prompted the authors of Samuel and Kings to tell their stories of the prophets. Whether or not the stories appear credible or historical, whether or not the prophets were in fact as they are described, and did in fact do as is reported of them in these tales, the writers of the stories displayed a noble spirit.

One more note and we can leave these third person narratives about the prophets. This note looks ahead to a later chapter. Perhaps the finest of all the stories about the prophets is the little book of Jonah—a story from beginning to end—one beautiful piece of fiction which says nothing at all about the historical prophet Jonah but a very great deal indeed about the author of the story. We notice it here because it fits formally into the present context, but we notice it only in passing because we will want to consider it at length in the spot where its message has pertinence.

THE AUTOBIOGRAPHICAL FORM

Now we move from third person to first person stories—from tales told about the prophets to memoirs of prophets, their own records of what they did and said, to the rare but precious occasions when the prophet writes: "I beheld the Lord seated on a throne high and lifted up"—"O that my head were water and my eyes a fount of tears!"—"Heal me, O Lord, that I may be healed!"

To achieve the transition from biography to autobiography consider the seventh chapter of Amos. It contains both types of narrative, and both probably reliable, though not without difficulties. We started to translate the third person narrative a few pages back. Here now is the whole story. Listen for the places where the narrator (whoever that is) lets Amos speak, and notice what Amos says when his words are quoted. Also do not be surprised at a change in tense in a familiar expression and an unexpected translation of an oft-quoted sentence. Probably Amos never said "I am not a prophet or the son of a prophet." That would not have made sense in the context. As the Jewish Publication Society translation correctly interprets it, this is probably what he said: "I was not a prophet or the son of a prophet"—and he meant: "I was as yet not serving as a prophet—I was otherwise employed, until God took me from my flocks and said—Go, prophesy!"

Here is the third person narrative which contains Amos's confrontation with, and his reply to Amaziah:

> Amaziah, the priest of Beth-El, sent word to Jeroboam the king of Israel saying: "Amos has conspired against you in the midst of Israel; the land cannot contain all his words. For so Amos has spoken: 'Jeroboam will die by the sword and Israel must be exiled from its land.' "
>
> Amaziah then said to Amos: "Seer! Go! Find refuge in the land of Judah. Earn your living there, and there prophesy. But prophesy no more at Beth-El, because it is a royal sanctuary and seat of government."
>
> But Amos replied and said to Amaziah: "I was not serving as a prophet nor trained as a prophet; I was occupied as a herdsman and

nipper of sycomore fruit when the Lord took
me from my flock and when the Lord said
to me: Go! Prophesy to My people Israel.
So now hear the word of the Lord! You say:
'You shall not prophesy to Israel, and you
shall not preach to the house of Isaac.' Therefore thus the Lord has said: 'Your wife will
ply the harlot's trade in the city, your sons
and daughters will fall before the sword, your
land will be distributed by lot, and you yourself will die in an unclean land, and yes, Israel
must be exiled from its land' " (7:10-17).

It is a concise and tightly packed narrative and it reveals
about as much as anyone can want to know about the
prophet Amos. Much could be said about this narrative but
we are interested here especially in its form. The narrator, as
we have noted, is not himself one of the characters involved
in this dramatic confrontation. He is not Amaziah or Jeroboam, or Amos. He speaks about Amaziah and Jeroboam and
Amos. He tells that "Amaziah sent word to Jeroboam saying:
Amos has conspired against you." "Amaziah then said to
Amos." "But Amos replied to Amaziah." The narrator is
none of these; he is an unnamed fourth party—a reporter
close enough to the principals to know the event, and,
judging by the way he tells the story, closest to the prophet.
Does it not seem that Amos had in this narrator a disciple—
even like Jeremiah's Baruch, in a later century, and like
Elisha's Gehazi in an earlier one—each disciple prepared to
tell his master's story? Isaiah, too, speaks of disciples, but his
disciples appear to have been more successful in preserving
(and supplementing?) his prophetic words than in narrating
his biography.

THE "CALL" OF AMOS

The hypothetical disciple of Amos, or at any rate the author
of this narrative quotes the words of his principals. And the

most interesting of these are the words of Amos concerning his call:

> I was not serving as a prophet nor trained as
> a prophet; I was occupied as a herdsman and
> nipper of sycomore fruit when the Lord took
> me from my flock and when the Lord said to
> me: Go! Prophesy to My people Israel!

Amos was going about his business, minding his herd, when the Lord took him and said: Go! Prophesy! These quoted words of Amos say in the tightest possible form what one prophet after another relates in what is usually a first person narrative, the circumstances of his being summoned to prophesy—the experience of a call—his consecration as prophet. To Amaziah, according to this third person narrative in Chapter 7, Amos said simply: "The Lord took me—He *took* me and said Go! Prophesy!" But in five other paragraphs of first person narrative Amos tells in the form of a five step vision just how the Lord "took" him, and in a superb poetic bit he describes the irrepressible urgency of the call.

The vision is arranged in five steps, each beginning with the words "So the Lord showed me," and each moving a step nearer the brink of Israel's doom, and each more compellingly pressing Amos to sound the alarm. These are Amos 7:1–3; 7:4–6; 7:7–8; 8:1–3 and 9:1–4. In such fashion God *took* him and sent him on his prophetic way. God left Amos no alternative; the prophet had to prophesy.

A prophet's need to speak is nowhere more forcefully stated than it is in the following words of Amos. In a series of eight analogies Amos works up to the climax of the ninth, and the total effect of his argument is the conclusion that the prophet's response to God his master is little less than automatic—a reflex comparable to the human reflex of fear.

> Do two find each other [he asks]
>   without pre-arrangement?
> Does a lion roar in the forest
>   unless he has taken prey?

Does a young lion roar in his lair
  unless he has made a kill?
Does a bird fall to the earth
  unless he is caught in a snare?
Does a trap spring up from the ground
  not triggered by a victim?
If an alarm is blown in a city
  is a people not terrified?
Does disaster befall a city
  if God has not formed it?
When a lion has roared
  who can control his fear?

Now the climax:

When the Lord God has spoken
  who can refrain from prophecy? (3:3–6, 8)

Amaziah had told Amos to keep quiet, or at any rate to go away from Beth-El and leave them alone. Whether Amos said to Amaziah what we have just heard him say, or whether thinking of his encounter with Amaziah at Beth-El he merely thought and recorded these words, the effect of them is that neither Amaziah nor any human power can command his silence. Like the reflex of fear, the need to speak is beyond a man's control. When God has spoken "who can refrain from prophecy?"

4

What Makes a Prophet

THE AUTOBIOGRAPHICAL MATERIAL IN THE PROPHETS IS VARIED, but most of it is by its very nature intimate. The narrator is relating an unshared experience, something that took place privately between him and God. He is the only man who can tell of it because he saw and heard what no other heard or saw. Only he can say "I saw," or "He showed me," "I heard" or "To me came this word of God." Some of the chapters of Ezekiel form a sizable exception as regards this intimacy, but it remains true that the autobiographical matter consists largely of auditions and visions. And among the visions the *prophetic call* occupies a prominent place.

THE CALL TO PROPHECY

Reserving Ezekiel for a later chapter let us here look especially at the consecration vision of the different prophets as they have reported it. We have already looked briefly at the call of Amos. The pattern of the vision or call is fairly regular. There are features which consistently recur. We shall focus on four of these features. They are:

First, that the prophet becomes aware of a mission. He knows that he is being *sent*. God tells him to *go*.

Second, that before he can go he must overcome a natural sense of inadequacy or unwillingness.

Third, that he understands his business to be communication. He is sent to speak for God, to say what God wants said.

Fourth, that he is fully aware of the magnitude of his task, conscious that communication is a difficult business.

An example will make this pattern clear. The four features are discernible in the opening chapter of Jeremiah. Here is a translation of the relevant parts of that chapter (verses 4–10 and 17–19, with some few phrases omitted; see Blank, *Jeremiah: Man and Prophet*, pp. 73f.):

> I received the word of the Lord:
>> Before I shaped you in the womb I knew you;
>>> before you went from the womb I adopted you;
>>> I designated you a prophet . . . .
> And I said:
>> Alas, Lord God! I know not how to speak,
>>> being merely a lad.
> And the Lord said to me:
>> Do not say: "I am a lad";
>>> for, wherever I send you you shall go,
>>> and whatsoever I command you you shall speak.
>> Do not fear . . . them,
>>> for I am with you to save you.
>>> It is the Lord speaking.
> And the Lord put forth His hand and touched my mouth.
> And the Lord said to me:
>> Lo, I have put My words in your mouth.
>>> See, I have designated you today [a prophet] . . .
>> To root out and tear down,
>>> and to lay waste and destroy,
>>> to rebuild and to replant.
>>> . . . Gird up your loins,
>>> get up and say to them
>>> all that I charge you.
>> Do not be discouraged by them
>>> or I will break you before them.
>> But I, lo, I make you this day as a fortified city,
>>> as an iron pillar and as walls of bronze
>>> over against the whole land,

> The kings of Judah and her princes,
>> her priests and the people of the land.
> If they fight with you they will not succeed
>> for I am with you to save you.
> It is the Lord speaking.

There it is—the whole pattern of the prophet's call in first person narrative form ("I received . . . ," "And I said . . .").

THE FIRST FEATURE

First: God tells him to *go*. Jeremiah's awareness of his mission comes early in the vision: "Wherever I send you you shall go." The key word is "Go." In one prophet's call after another we hear it.

To Moses God said: "Go, now; I will send you to Pharaoh." When Moses then said to God: Who am I that I should go to Pharaoh and that I should bring the children of Israel out of Egypt? God simply said: I will be with you (Exod. 3:10–12).

We remember what (according to his biographer) Amos said of his call: I was not serving as a prophet nor trained as a prophet; I was occupied as a herdsman and nipper of sycomore fruit when the Lord took me from my flock—and the Lord said to me: Go! Prophesy to My people Israel.

Isaiah heard the Lord saying: Whom shall I send, and who will go for us? And Isaiah said: I am here; send me. And God said: Go! (Isa. 6:8f.)

We observe, too, what God said to Jeremiah: Do not say: "I am a lad"; for, wherever I send you you shall go, and whatever I command you you shall speak.

Ezekiel was given words to eat, and then God said to him: Go; go to the house of Israel and speak with My words to them (Ezek. 3:4).

Also to Jonah came the word of the Lord saying: Arise, go

to Nineveh, that great city, and proclaim against it (Jonah 1:2).

And according to the tradition, at the very beginning of our history as a people, to Abraham, who in this passage is a symbol for this people—to him too God said Go! "Go from your country and from your kindred, and from your father's house, to the land that I will show you, and I will make of you a great nation, and I will bless you and make your name great; and you shall be a blessing . . . In you shall all the families of the earth be blessed" (Gen. 12:1-3).

So this is a common theme in the visions of the prophets, this sense of being called and sent. God has urged him and the man must go. God will not reprove him as arrogant, God will not accuse him of the fault of *hubris*—of reaching too high like Icarus or Prometheus; God will not think of him as a rival. God will frown only on his tardy response, God will blame the man only if he is too ready to rest on his status quo and fails to reach, God thinks of him as a responsible agent and partner. He is not jealous of man—God is not jealous *of* man, He is jealous *for* man.

We might readily move from the individual to the species man. But our interest is in the single prophet with his urgent sense that he has been sent, that he is a *meshullach*, a man with a mission to others. This theme of mission has remained through the centuries and we will want to speak of it again at the end of this study. It is perhaps the most important thing the prophets have bequeathed to us, the thought that a man, or a people, may be divinely sent.

THE SECOND FEATURE

Now look back at Jeremiah's call and the second common feature, the prophet's hesitant awe, his *reluctance*, unwillingness, sense of inadequacy, which, of course, he must overcome before he can go where he is sent and speak what he must speak.

When in his vision Jeremiah heard God's summons, in wonder he exclaimed: "Alas, Lord God! I know not how to speak, being a mere lad." "Lad" is *na'ar* in Hebrew; it does not mean boy or child. In fact it does not say anything very clearly about Jeremiah's age at the time—except perhaps that he was not a *zaken*, a bearded elder. It says more about his state of mind. It is his way of saying: I am not worthy, not equal to the task.

Solomon spoke in similar terms when he was called to kingship: "I am a young lad and do not know the ways of the world" (I Kings 3:5ff.). Then God comforted him in a dream and he went on to do quite well for himself and for Israel.

Like him too spoke Gideon among the judges, when he was called to military leadership. Turning to him the Lord said: "Go (as he said to prophets, God also said to Gideon: Go) by reason of this strength of yours and deliver Israel from the power of Midian. Have I not sent you?" And he replied, "Ah, Lord, by what means can I save Israel? My family is the poorest of the tribe of Menasseh and I am the least member of my household." But the Lord said to him: "I will be with you and you will smite Midian as you might a single man" (Judg. 6:14ff.).

We remember too how Moses demurred: "Who am I that I should go to Pharaoh and that I should bring the children of Israel out of Egypt?"—how he protested and how he was convinced.

In the gleaming vision of Isaiah this feature is also not lacking. He has seen the Lord on His high throne, His robe filling the Temple, six winged seraphim waiting on Him. He has heard the threefold proclamation of God's holiness. He has felt the thresholds trembling, and in dismay and awe he cries: "Ah me, I am undone, for I am a man of unclean lips dwelling among a people of unclean lips." The coal to his lips overcame his reserve (Isa. 6).

It is not always present—this hesitance—but it is attested by enough examples to establish it as a feature of the pattern of the prophetic call. The pattern is psychologically sound. A sense of mission is one thing; being prepared to undertake a mission is another. A man must overcome a natural reticence, which may, but need not, be mixed with laziness or inertia. He must gather his self-respect and give up feeling small. This must happen before a man can respond like Isaiah: "I am here. Send me." It is not strange that the dedication of a man, his commitment to a cause, should follow in this fashion on the struggle. Only when a man—only when a people—has won through to self-appreciation is he—or it—in fact large enough for the task.

THE THIRD FEATURE

A third characteristic of the call is almost always present in the pattern. It concerns the function of the prophet, what it is he understands his business to be. He knows himself called to *speak* for God. He knows that God wants to use his mouth.

Scholars differ among themselves about the original meaning of the Hebrew word for prophet, the noun *nabi*. When the verb related to this noun occurs in the Bible it means "to behave like a prophet"—and so the Hebrew verb is of no use at all in determining the meaning of the noun. We are dealing with probabilities, but the most probable opinion is that *nabi* originally meant just what we have been talking about—one who has been called—one whom a god has summoned. The word is probably older than the Bible and probably not originally a Hebrew word but one borrowed from Akkadian. The meaning "one who has been divinely called" well suits the biblical usage.

When we turn from the Hebrew term *nabi* to the English word "prophet" we have a different story. The English word was borrowed from Greece. Originally a prophet there was one who spoke for a god, interpreting the oracles. The oracles in Greece required interpretation; they were sounds unlike human speech. Without prophets the gods could not communicate with men. Prophets made the sounds intelligible. To the extent that the English word "prophet" retains this original meaning it pretty well describes the function of the Hebrew prophet as he conceived it in his call. He too thought of communication as his function.

Unfortunately the English word prophet has attracted to itself a different, less suitable meaning. Popularly it means, one who predicts future events. Now we will not deny that the Hebrew prophets predicted. They did indeed. It is wrong to say: "The prophets were not foretellers, they were forthtellers." They were both. And that fancy formula is misleading. They said what they thought the future held in store. They were not always right but they predicted much and often.

Only, it was not because they predicted that they were called prophets; it was because they spoke for God. The visions reveal that they clearly understood this to be their business and this is the third feature in the pattern of the call.

One prophet after another refers to his mouth, tongue, lips, that is to say his organs of speech, as dedicated to the service of his God. We recall the reference in Jeremiah's vision: "And the Lord put forth His hand and touched my mouth," says Jeremiah. "And the Lord said to me: Lo, I have put My words in your mouth."

We remember Isaiah's experience as he tells of it in connection with his call. After his cry of dismay: "Ah me!" he says:

> Then one of the seraphs flew to me holding
> a coal taken with tongs from the altar,
> touched it to my mouth and said: "Lo this
> has touched your lips; your guilt has turned
> aside and your sin is forgiven." And then
> when I heard the voice of the Lord saying:

> "Whom shall I send and who will go for us?"
> I said: "I am here. Send me" (Isa. 6:6–8).

We think too of Ezekiel's vision only a little later than
Jeremiah's—how the "glory of God" came to him as an
elaborate apparition, raised him when he fell down in adora-
tion, and said:

> Heed what I tell you, son of man, . . . open
> your mouth and eat what I give you. Then I
> looked and lo! a hand was extended towards
> me, and in it a scroll. And He unrolled it for
> me and it was inscribed on both sides with
> lamentation and moaning and woe. And He
> said to me: Son of man, eat what you find.
> Eat this scroll! then go, speak to the house of
> Israel. So I opened my mouth and He fed me
> this scroll. And He said to me: Son of man,
> fill your belly with this scroll which I give
> you. So I ate it and it tasted as sweet as
> honey. And He said to me: Son of man, go,
> come to the house of Israel and speak My
> words to them (Ezek. 2:8–3:4).

Thus graphically Ezekiel describes the use God makes of his
mouth.

And not the three major prophets Isaiah, Jeremiah, Ezekiel
only, but several others tell of the dedication of their mouth
to God's service. Amos is less obvious than these three but
we remember his words: "When the Lord God has spoken
who can refrain from prophecy?" Moses and Aaron and
Balaam and Micaiah and, in the Second Isaiah, the servant
figure present the same picture.

See what they say: The imported prophet Balaam, in the
Book of Numbers (22:38 and elsewhere) patiently explains to
Balak the king of Moab: "Now that I have come to you, can
I (for myself) say anything at all? That word only which
God puts in my mouth can I speak."

The Hebrew prophet Micaiah in the twenty-second chapter of First Kings—not to be confused with Micah among the Twelve—this Micaiah had the same news for the kings of Israel and Judah: "As the Lord lives, only what the Lord says to me can I say" (vs. 14). And when rival prophets led by Zedekiah brought an opposing message, he insisted: "The Lord has put a spirit of falsehood in the mouth of all these prophets." It is perhaps natural, also, that since the words of one man's mouth were contested by the mouth of another, the blow aimed at Micaiah should land on his jaw, designed as it was to silence him (vss. 23f.).

Prophet-like, the "servant of God," who was no prophet but a symbol for Israel, speaks of mouth and tongue and word: "God made my mouth a sharp sword," "God gave me the tongue of disciples," "He stirs up a word in the morning" (Isa. 49:2; 50:4).

In Midian, when God prepared to send Moses forth as His prophet, and Moses objected: "Who am I that I should go to Pharaoh?" and then more specifically: "I am not a man of words and have not been . . . but am heavy of mouth and tongue," God rebuked Moses with a pointed reminder: "Who gave man a mouth and who makes one dumb? . . . Go, and I will be with your mouth and instruct you what to say" (Exod. 4:10–12).

What is probably another source in the same chapter in Exodus admits that Moses has a speech difficulty and substitutes Aaron for Moses as prophet because, God says: "He can certainly speak"; "and you will speak to him and put words in his mouth and I will be with your mouth and with his and I will tell you what to do. And he shall speak for you to the people and he shall be mouth to you and you shall be God to him" (Exod. 4:14–16). In one of the most revealing passages among these many, because Aaron serves as mouth to Moses, God calls him Moses' "prophet": "And Aaron your brother will be your prophet [nabi is the word]. You will speak to him all that I command you, and Aaron your brother will speak to Pharaoh" (Exod. 7:1f.). Nothing could be clearer. According to biblical usage, being a prophet means letting another use your mouth for speaking. God used the prophet's mouth. The prophet is the means God uses to communicate. Communication is the prophet's business.

THE FOURTH FEATURE

But *communication is difficult* and the life of a prophet is not easy. We find many bitter words spoken by such prophets as Isaiah, Jeremiah and Ezekiel which attest to the fact that they regarded themselves as failures. We have still to consider in a later chapter whether indeed they failed, or why they failed if indeed they did, but that they thought they failed they bitterly testify—and this is the fourth feature of the prophetic call.

Perhaps it is Ezekiel who says it most clearly and in far from amiable terms. It is as though he were quite out of patience with a witless and obdurate public. After Ezekiel has eaten the scroll and received his instructions to speak to the house of Israel, according to his report, this is what God said to him: "But the house of Israel will not be willing to listen to you, because they are not willing to listen to Me, because all the house of Israel are numbskulls and fatheads" (Ezek. 3:7). Ezekiel is known for his vigorous language.

The Second Isaiah is equally clear though less vituperative. He has God say of Israel in Exile: "Hear you that are deaf, you that are blind look and see! Who so blind as my servant, or deaf as my commissioned messenger?" (Isa. 42:18f.).

Ezekiel and the Second Isaiah say it clearly enough: the prophets had trouble communicating with their people. They say it clearly but others say it also.

We remember Jeremiah's vision and God's words to him there: "Do not fear them." "Do not be discouraged by them or I will break you before them . . . I make you this day as a fortified city, as an iron pillar and as walls of bronze . . . If they fight with you they will not succeed, for I am with you to save you. It is the Lord speaking." This is perhaps a little harder to understand than it seems superficially. Why does God thus fortify the young Jeremiah already at the time of his call with promises of support? Why should Jeremiah fear his people, be discouraged by them before he starts, have early premonitions of failure? Two answers are possible— and there may be truth in both of them. One is that Jeremiah knew from the experience of his eighth century predecessors, from the lives of men like Amos, Hosea, Micah and Isaiah, that his words would not be well received—knew this because what he had to say was not substantially different from their demonstrably unpopular words. The other answer is that some of his own experience went into the shaping of this first-person narrative. But if this is his call to prophecy, at the very beginning of his career, one may ask, how much experience of his own could have gone into its shaping? And the objection is proper, and the only way around it is the assumption that Jeremiah did not at once write down his vision and that when, after some years had passed, he did put it into words, the agony of those years of struggle and frustration found expression there too.

This is not a wild assumption; there are other reasons in the Jeremiah story for believing that a later event prompted Jeremiah to put down on record this earlier vision. Moreover, the same assumption is the only adequate explanation for an extremely awkward bit of theology in the consecration vision of the prophet Isaiah. After the coal had prepared that prophet's lips and he had volunteered "Here I am. Send me," he received his orders and they are strange indeed. He was told to say to his people: "Hear, without understanding; see, with no comprehension." And his orders continue in the same dismaying vein: "Dull this people's mind, plug up their ears, blindfold them. Otherwise they might see, hear, understand, and so repent and be cured." If one finds it hard to understand this passage, that is not strange. The only way to make sense of it is to employ the assumption already mentioned—namely that a heap of anguish intervened between the time when Isaiah received his call and commission as prophet and the time late in his life when he actually put that experience down for the record, and that the anguish of those years of service shaped this bitter passage. This is not theology and it is not to be treated as such. In these ironic sentences Isaiah only pays his respects to human nature, limited, as it seems to him, by a deadening infatuation—and his words poorly conceal the agony of his repeated experience of frustration.

Why Certain Prophets Found Communication Difficult

Wᴴʏ ᴡᴇʀᴇ ᴇᴢᴇᴋɪᴇʟ ᴀɴᴅ ᴊᴇʀᴇᴍɪᴀʜ ᴀɴᴅ ᴛʜᴇ ᴏᴛʜᴇʀ ᴘʀᴏᴘʜᴇᴛs frustrated in such fashion? Why did their people not hear? Why could they not hear?

We have been roving over quite a bit of territory. Let us narrow the field somewhat. When we speak of "prophets" now for a while let us omit the Elijahs and Elishas, Moses and Daniel and all the others except for only six well-known people: the constellation of four eighth century prophets, Amos, Hosea, Micah and Isaiah, plus two in the seventh century, Jeremiah and Ezekiel, two who lived to see the destruction of the Temple in 587 ʙ.ᴄ.ᴇ.—those six for now, and especially Isaiah among them. Later our interest will shift to the prophets in and after the Babylonian Exile and what they thought—but now only the earlier six among the literary prophets.

Why were these six prophets not able to get across to their people? Why could their people not hear them? To answer the question simply, the people could not hear these prophets because these prophets said what the people did not like to hear, because these prophets made people feel uncomfortable.

If we were looking for a modern analogy we would not

compare these prophets to the pastors of today. A pastoral ministry is a noble calling; it is fine to be a shepherd of souls. But a pastor is not a prophet. Prophets (and now we mean these six, and while Jerusalem still stood)—these prophets were not concerned with contentment; implanting peace of mind was not their goal—at any rate not their immediate goal. Men would not come to them for comfort in personal sorrow, guidance in confusion, reassurance in a crisis of self-hate; men would not come to the prophets as to a rabbi or minister for any of these warm human contacts. Those prophets were no pastors.

They were "disturbers of the peace"; they did not soothe but irritate. Today we put such men in jail. If a preacher were to talk to his congregation the way these prophets spoke to their people, pointing his finger and stepping on toes, he would soon not have a congregation. We have to remember this when we teach the prophets to the young. When we tend to become over-enthusiastic we need to remind ourselves that the prophetic way is not an ingratiating way; it does not lead to success. One who follows that way may defeat the very purpose he pursues. Despite our awed admiration for the prophets we would not like to have one of them as a neighbor. We could not live with a prophet; he would make us thoroughly uncomfortable. We would rather not be bothered, and a prophet around the corner would be bothersome indeed.

PROPHETS ASKED QUESTIONS

Prompted by God prophets raised questions about what people had always believed; they cast doubts on what seemed axiomatic. They were fanatical in their challenge to accustomed ways and cherished beliefs.

THE COVENANT AND ITS COROLLARIES

Much of what those prophets challenged is covered by what we could call the then current interpretation of the *covenant*. The word "covenant" (in Hebrew *berit*) is a common word in the Bible. A covenant is about the same as a contract; it is an agreement between two parties. The biblical covenant in question is a presumed agreement between Israel and God. ("Presumed" or "historical" is not important—the tradition is enough.) There was, according to the Genesis story, a very early covenant not merely between God and Israel, in the person of Abraham, then Isaac and then Jacob, but also between God and all flesh—the covenant sealed by a rainbow after the flood in the presence of all who came with Noah from the ark. And, of course, there was the tradition of the covenant at Sinai.

The covenant idea is pervasive—found everywhere in the Hebrew Bible. There is a great deal of merit in it and it occupies an important place in Jewish ethics. Usually in the Bible the covenant is expressed as a formula, the words addressed by God to Israel: "You shall be My people and I will be your God."

Now there is one thing about the covenant idea which we must look at closely: the obvious fact that just as it takes two to make an argument it takes two to make an agreement; implicit in the covenant formula is the sense of mutual obligation. The rainbow covenant with Noah includes a simple set of laws, apparently the human obligation corresponding to God's undertaking (Gen. 9:1–17). In the several records of the covenant between God and Israel at Sinai (*e.g.*, Exod. 19:5–8), Israel's duties are specified—duties matching privileges. According to the Sinai tradition God undertook to care for his people, to give them secure possession of the land, long life and plenty, assuming, of course, that they in turn would live up to their part of the agreement: faithfully serving God in a prescribed fashion. This is the essence of the covenant concept: that a bill of duties balances a bill of rights. And our common western religious heritage of duty owes much to that ancient covenant tradition.

But the covenant idea contains elements also of potential danger. Interpret it loosely or interpret it wrongly and it loses all of its ethical import. Think of it as a promise or commitment on the part of only one of the two parties, and if that one is God then the other party (Israel or "all flesh") is left with no responsibilities to set against the benefits, left with nothing but the passive attitude of receptivity, a supine drinking-in of divine beneficence. A people may come to take too much for granted, may count on "Providence" and do so with confidence, remembering, because it is comfortable to do so, God's obligations and growing quite careless of their own, resting on the assumed indulgence and benevolence of God. So doing, they put new meaning in an old word and expect God under the ancient covenant, now no longer a covenant but simply a promise, to assume the total responsibility. That is one danger that lurked in the idea of the covenant.

Also, good as it is, the covenant idea contained a second potential danger. Men may admit that they have an obligation but as concerns this duty they may be thinking of something quite inadequate if not indeed irrelevant. If the human obligation which has been taken on to balance the divine undertaking is conceived in purely formal, ceremonial, or ritual terms, have men really done their part? From strictures which the prophets levelled at their people we may conclude that in those times the people had succumbed to this danger. The picture is not pretty as those prophets draw it. The popular religion appears as wholly given to rituals and ceremonial observances, visits to sanctuaries, prayers and music, donations and sacrifices. The pilgrimage to a shrine was a picnic, a holiday trip for the family. And as for the frequent sacrifices, after God had received His share on the altar the roasted animal was served up as at a cook-out to the prayerful worshippers, who then smugly assumed that they had performed their religious duties and were deserving of God's protection and His blessing. There seems to have been no awareness on the part of those to whom these prophets spoke that other duties than these might better comport with the nature of Israel's God.

Two things more! The popular interpretation of the covenant current in the days of these prophets was responsible for a sense of blissful security. Everyone in the kingdom of Israel was utterly sure "it could not happen there." The covenant meant that Jerusalem was an impregnable fortress, not, to be sure, because of the thickness of its walls, not even because of the valor of its defenders, but just because of that special relationship which had grown up between Israel and the God whose Temple stood on Zion's hill. Zion lay securely sheltered in the shadow of God's wings.

Also a corollary of the covenant idea was the cherished notion of "the day of the Lord." People were not merely saying about Jerusalem: "It cannot happen here." They were mumbling to themselves as well "Just you wait" and "You ain't seen nothing yet." *The day*, the day of the Lord, awesome and final, would come and strike with calamitous defeat all the armies of all the nations that ever waged war against Zion; God would be victorious on that day and His people triumphant. That would be the day!

These are some of the pink clouds on which the people of Israel were drifting in the days of some of the prophets. And it seemed to be the business of those prophets in particular—of those six at least—and before the Exile—it seemed to be their divinely appointed task simply to challenge the validity of these comfortable popular assumptions. Platitudes were their enemies and valiantly they battled against them. They dared and they disturbed.

ISAIAH THE CHALLENGER

They dared question the then current interpretation of the covenant. They did not question the covenant tradition itself; they operated within its frame. There had indeed been an arrangement between God and Israel; on that they agreed. But it was a proper covenant, a conditional contract, with obligations on both sides, they would insist. If one of the parties defaulted the other went free, and the covenant was voided. They called a covenant a covenant, not a unilateral divine commitment. That is the meaning of Isaiah's parable of the vineyard, that Israel had failed to do its part, that the covenant is void and God is removing His protective care.

> Let me sing about my friend,
>   a song about my loved one and his vineyard:
> My friend had a vineyard
>   on a fertile slope.
> And he cultivated it and cleared away the stones,
>   and he set out cuttings of a noble vine.
> Also he built a citadel in its midst
>   and hewed out a winevat
> Hoping that it would produce proper fruit,
>   but the grapes were wild.

What must follow? God will remove the protecting hedge, withhold His rain, and make an end of His now worthless vineyard.

That is the parable; and what does it mean?

> The vineyard of the Lord of Hosts
>   is the house of Israel
> And the men of Judah
>   are His pleasant plantation.

> But when He hoped for justice,
>   oh! the destruction!
> He hoped for acts of righteousness,
>   but oh! the cries of pain (Isa. 5:1–7).

The conclusion of this vivid metaphor leads over to a second observation. But to complete the first: Those prophets—here Isaiah, but others as well—dared to say that the covenant arrangement between God and His people was conditional, and in fact—things being as they were—quite temporary; and these prophets disturbed the whole people which had come to think of itself as chosen and as privileged, and to think of God as their "portion," their possession forever. Jerusalem was their proud fortress. On Zion's hill stood the national shrine holy to their God, a symbol of His need for them. In God they trusted with an explicit trust and took His care for granted. Isaiah challenged their confident ease and denied that God was chained to any nation. He declared God's independence and disturbed a lot of people.

The metaphor of the vineyard ended with the words: "When He hoped for justice, oh! destruction! He hoped for acts of righteousness, but oh! the cries of pain!" And these words suggest a second of the ways that Isaiah and others questioned the popular interpretation of the covenant. For those who admitted that the arrangement with God obligated them to do something in return for His beneficence, but interpreted their obligations in terms of rituals: pilgrimages and sacrifices, hymns and prayers, Isaiah had a second denial. This was not what God wanted at all; God looked for something else instead.

> What do your many sacrifices mean to Me?
>   God asks.
> I am fed up with the roasting rams
>   and the grease of fattened beasts. . . .
> When you present yourselves before Me
>   who wants this of you—
>   trampling My precincts? . . .

> Your newmoon ceremonies and your assemblies—
>   I hate them;
> I find them a burden;
>   they weary Me.
> When you stretch out your hands
>   I look the other way,
> And when you pray long prayers
>   I do not listen (Isa. 1:11–12, 14–15a).

The people were not neglecting their religious duties; or at any rate they were doing what they thought God had asked of them. Regularly three times a year, if not also on newmoon days and Sabbaths, they visited His sanctuary. And when they appeared before Him they were not empty handed. They returned to Him some of His bounty, bringing grain and beasts for His altars, and there with outstretched hands they sang His praises. But Isaiah saw it otherwise. He regarded this interpretation of the covenant requirements in terms of ceremony as nothing short of a religious aberration.

There is more to this passage than a denial. This negation does not stand alone; Isaiah continues in the lines that follow with a powerful affirmation, a specific listing of what instead of the motions of worship, God does demand of His people in return for His bounty—but that is a matter for a later chapter. This thought for the present: Isaiah and his kind of prophet dared to say that when God brought Israel from Egypt He did not demand that they build Him a sanctuary and offer on its altar bulls and rams—and they disturbed all of the people who thought that their God had done so, and that with the savor of their roasts they were pleasing God.

As we have seen, reliance on the covenant meant confidence that Jerusalem was a high tower, secure from all foes. But the prophetic challenge of the covenant called into question also this axiom. Isaiah repeatedly denied that Zion was safe. Quite the contrary! He was convinced that the Assyrian would lay siege to the city, breach its walls, burn its buildings and slaughter or take captive its inhabitants. He thought of

Assyria as the agent of God and it seemed to Isaiah as though God himself were at work. So he could speak for God and say to Zion:

> I will camp against you. . .
>   I will shut you in. . . .
> I will raise siege works against you (Isa. 29:3).

He could talk of God's attack on Jerusalem and say:

> As the lion growls,
>   the young lion over its prey,
> [And] though there be assembled against him
>   a full band of shepherds,
> He fears not their shouting
>   and is not diverted by their tumult,
> Just so [that is to say, with just such unde-
>   viating purposefulness] the Lord of Hosts
>   will come down
> To lay siege to Zion and her hill (Isa. 31:4).

Isaiah sees Jerusalem's God personally conducting the Assyrian siege of His city (strange behavior for a city's God!) and giving victory to the foe. And perhaps nothing that he said disturbed his people more than this.

Incidentally and significantly, this view is one of those which distinguishes the historical from the legendary Isaiah. Those stories about Isaiah which appear in his chapters 36–39 but which as we have noted seem originally to have been at home where they can still be found as well, near the end of Second Kings, those stories represent Isaiah—they misrepresent him—as espousing the popular interpretation of the covenant, taking it to mean that at all costs God would shelter, protect, shield and spare His chosen city Zion, His residence. This is the storybook prophet, not the Isaiah whom we know from other parts of his book, from his first person narratives and his prophetic utterances. The distinction we have drawn between the third person sources in Isaiah and the others has application here. It is time to forget the textbook cliché which teaches that a mellowed Isaiah reversed himself near the end of his life and espoused the popular view that Jerusalem was impregnable.

And what was Isaiah's expectation as concerns the fabulous, future "day of the Lord"? "Remember," Moses had told them, "that you were enslaved in Egypt and the Lord your God brought you out of there with a strong hand and arm outstretched" (Deut. 5:15). "You shall indeed remember what the Lord your God did to Pharaoh and all Egypt," Moses had said, "the great trials of strength which you witnessed, the signs and wonders and the strong hand and arm outstretched with which the Lord your God brought you thence" (Deut. 7:18f.), and they remembered. They recalled as well how "David came to Baal Perazim and defeated the Philistines there and said: The Lord gushed forth against my enemies like the bursting forth of water" (II Sam. 5:20). Nor did they forget that their God had "put to rout the kings of Canaan," responding to Joshua's spell: "O sun, stand still in Gibeon, and moon in the Vale of Ajalon," as it is written: "And the sun stopped at the meridian and for a whole day it did not hurry on to set" (Josh. 10:10, 13). They were mindful that David had taken for them the Jebusite fortress Jerusalem to make of it his capital (II Sam. 5:6–10). There his son Solomon built the Temple and lodged the ark, the ancient symbol of the mighty presence of the Lord. All portents were good and what had been could be again. A people with a God who shaped their history by His will and worked saving miracles with casual ease could only triumph when the day of decision dawned. That brilliant dawn would mean defeat for their enemies, victory for God and Israel.

The prophet Isaiah did not share in this sanguine popular expectation. Like his people he saw their God at work in history, but unlike them he foresaw no national triumph. The people had not returned to Him that smote them and Isaiah had a dim view of their future. God's hand was stretched out still (Isa. 9:12,11). What He would do for His stubbornly unresponsive people would seem "wondrous," "alien," "strange" and "terrifying"—all of these adjectives are Isaiah's (29:14; 28:19,21). God's strong arm outstretched would fall not on the foes at Israel's throat but heavily on His own thick-headed people. That "day of the Lord" would be God's day, not theirs. He would show Himself their Lord.

Those are some among the daring and disturbing and incredible things that Isaiah said. His words shielded no sacred dogma, left no inherited belief unchallenged. His denials hacked off a cherished notion here, a cultivated delusion there, and bared the bones of reality. His was a mind not lulled to sleep by any comforting wish-thought but alertly open to those impulses which we call divine, a mind indeed that was reaching out to find and clutch such affirmations as might deliver his people from looming evil. He was, as we have said, a persistent, fanatical, questioner of the always believed.

Isaiah was not, indeed, alone in his challenge and we will see the extent to which other prophets among the six shared his heresies. His was not the only voice raised to proclaim them, but he says enough to help us find the answer to our question: Why did these prophets find communication next to impossible? Why must they think of themselves as failures? Why did they not get across?

It was in the nature of things that men would not listen to them. Consider what happens when a person disturbs our peace, makes us uncomfortable by asking us to think or, in fact, to rethink what we have always been able to take for granted and have built our lives on as their foundation. What do we do to a prop-knocker-out-from-under? We do what the Hebrew people did to their prophets then—mostly we ignore them.

How Not to Hear
and Yet to Hear

THERE ARE TWO WAYS TO DEAL WITH CRACKPOTS AND BOTH ARE in common use. We may meet the threat with violence, or we may look the other way. The first of these methods was not unknown in Bible times but the second was the more usual.

TAKING MEASURES TO SILENCE A PROPHET

The violence took the form of measures designed to shut the prophet up or to get rid of him. It is a legend with no shred of biblical support that Isaiah suffered a martyr's death, and this groundless rabbinic fantasy should be forgotten. There is no record of violence done to Isaiah; he was given the alternative treatment—he was ignored as we have noticed.

It is to Amos and Jeremiah and the less known prophet Uriah that we turn for illustrations of violence done to a prophet. Amaziah the priest at Beth-El said to Amos:

> Seer! Go for safety to the land of Judah and there earn your living, and prophesy there and not any more at Beth-El because it is the site of a royal sanctuary and a seat of government (7:12–13).

He sought to rid the Northern Kingdom (Israel) of this man because, as he interpreted the message, Amos was conspiring against King Jeroboam and the country was menaced by his words (vs. 10). With what appears to be a disguised threat ("go for safety"), the priest orders Amos off the precincts and out of the realm. He seeks to dam up the words by banning the speaker.

The life of Jeremiah is full of such confrontations, such threats of violence and violence itself. Here is a summary of this prophet's story:

> The narratives about Jeremiah, the biographical sections of his book . . . describe a prophet's desolating career. Peril and the experience of violence, indignity, and virtual banishment were the ingredients of his life. . . . He was accused and tried for a capital offense and though he obtained acquittal he was to hear of a like-minded prophet who, for the same offense, did not escape death. He spent years as an outcast and learned of the obliteration of his book. When a king ordered his arrest he had to prolong his hiding. Active again, he was taken and flogged and endured the worse pain of exposure in stocks. A rival prophet assaulted him, another wrote calumny and urged further violence. An official accused him falsely so that he was flogged again and imprisoned. Prison life threatened his health, confinement in the depths of a cistern threatened him with extinction. Delivered from that danger he yet remained under arrest. When his king suffered defeat, he was released, but only to be abducted to Egypt, to spend his last years as an émigré. (See *Jeremiah, Man and Prophet*, p. 61.)

This is a full and varied tabulation of deeds of violence done a prophet but it includes only the affronts to his body. What his spirit was made to suffer would fill another paragraph.

Significant in the list is the reference to the obliteration of Jeremiah's book. That is an interesting business, the royal burning of the one scroll on which Baruch had written the prophet's messages at Jeremiah's dictation. As we read the story (in Chapter 36) we get the feeling that the king had to do what he did—to slash the pages to shreds with a knife and throw them into the fire, and thus reduce the written words to ashes. He and his nobles were terrified and trembled so long as the words were there. Their peace returned only when the words dispersed with the smoke. Words in those days had substance and effective reality; they were power-laden and might produce calamity. In his message as well as his person Jeremiah passed as a menace to his society, and the violence done him and his book causes no wonder. His persecutors simply acted in the public interest.

Four biblical verses tell us all that we know about the scarcely known prophet Uriah. They also serve as his obituary. The four verses are appended to the story of the trial of Jeremiah (Chapter 26) and the event they describe seems to have followed on Jeremiah's acquittal. They say:

> Another man, Uriah . . . of Kiriath Yearim, prophesied in God's name, and prophesied of this city and of this land words much like those of Jeremiah. And the king Jehoiakim and all his warriors and all the princes feared his words and the king undertook to kill him. Uriah heard and fled for safety to Egypt, but the king Jehoiakim sent . . . men . . . to Egypt and they fetched Uriah away from Egypt and brought him to the king Jehoiakim, and he put him to the sword and cast his body on the people's graves (26:20–23).

This king dammed up the words by destroying the speaker.

So violence was done the prophets. That is not strange. What is strange is that examples are rare. Apparently the dread of the threatening word and the need to obliterate it along with the author was counterbalanced by a sense of awe and respect for the prophet's putative holiness and the realization, perhaps, that the man was only the implement or agent of communication and not in fact the author of the word he brought. Though they might destroy the prophet, his prompter would remain. Whatever the explanation, the fact is that among the six prophets—or seven if we add the little known Uriah—of the seven who brought almost the same message, only for Amos (to a limited extent), Jeremiah and Uriah is there found a record of physical violence done them. The person of the prophet enjoyed a certain measure of immunity.

LOOKING THE OTHER WAY

And people used a different method to shield themselves from the menace of the prophetic word. They said: We won't listen; and whatever little they may have heard, through evil mischance, they erased from their memories.

Is that not what we still do? Do we not, in our civilized way, employ more commonly the second method for dealing with disturbing thoughts? We isolate and seal them off, as an organism does a harmful invader. As the body seals off an infection, or tries to do so, the mind sets up a block in the way of an unwanted idea. This mental habit of men, this psychological trait, useful perhaps, or deadening, as the case may be, was the prophet's Sambatyon—the turbulent boundary he could not cross, the barrier he could not get over. This was the reason for his sense of frustration, the irritant that aroused his invective. This is why impatiently the prophet called his people deaf and blind, numbskulls, fat-heads, stubbornly brazen and stiff-necked. (Prophets were not complimenting their people when they called them stiff-necked.) This is why in one prophetic call after another, as we have noted, the prophet appears from the outset to antici-pate failure—if the discouragement is not in fact, as we have suggested, retrospective commentary on a life misspent—which comes to the same thing.

The question again and the answer: Why could the people not hear their prophets? Because what their prophets said made them uncomfortable. The prophets were questioning their axioms, disputing their time-honored, respectable no-tions, countering their cherished beliefs, shaking their foun-dations, shattering the structure of their faith. Yes, their prophets were disturbing a lot of people, both common and important.

It is because of what the prophets said that the prophets were not heard. Let us not underestimate the shock of their words. Their words were not insipid then. If today they sound vapid or tame, blame the passing of centuries, or blame the sickness of our time which robs all words of their primal strength and makes them mean everything at once and there-fore nothing at all. Such things as these six prophets said were wild and shocking. The daring thoughts which we have reviewed were challenging and fear-evoking. How to handle them? See only what you want to see, hear only what you choose to hear, learn only what you know already, reject what makes you uneasy, forget what upsets you. If you do not like being disturbed, do not listen. Say "Tosh!" and "Piffle!" and jeer at the speaker.

AND YET TO HEAR

Now observe. In spite of the forces that might well have silenced the Hebrew prophets, in spite of the overpowering temptation to ignore their needling words, there must have been those that heard. Otherwise we could not now after twenty-five centuries simply open a Bible and read the message, read all the terrifying and daring and disturbing words those prophets spoke. Obviously, the society that the prophets denounced could hear after all and they were just possibly more tolerant than their prophets. The people let their prophets say the things they said, and say them again and again and get away with it, usually, and survive, for the most part. Together with their prophets ancient Israel wrote a proud chapter in the history of tolerance. When they tried to silence the voices of challenge and dissent in their midst, they did not try too hard. They found the words menacing but they let them be heard. And more than this, they preserved them and passed them on as a cherished tradition.

When we ask how this could be, we find as a probable answer the fact that these prophets offered their words as the word of God. They came as messengers and said: "Thus says the Lord." In this manner they spoke, and they spoke with such assurance that men hesitated to disbelieve. The appropriate question is not "Why were the people inclined to believe their prophets?" but rather "How could the prophets speak with such convincing self-assurance? What was the source of their certainty that they spoke for God? How did the prophets know?"

HOW THE PROPHETS KNEW

If we were to ask a prophet how he knows that he is right he would have no difficulty telling us but we would have difficulty with his explanation. The trouble is that he would talk to us primarily of an unshared religious experience. Prophets based their authority solidly on their conviction that God had called them for His purpose. But no persons other than the prophets themselves were witnesses to that call. The prophet's call was not in the public domain.

Consider an example: the beginning of the Book of Ezekiel describes an event that occurred early in the course of Ezekiel's prophetic career. It is quite possible that many other people were there when it happened—an electric storm with dark billowing clouds of fantastic shifting shapes, flashes of lightning, crashing thunder and the sound of wind, sun-rays breaking through and a rainbow spectrum—anyone would have seen these sights and sounds if he stood with the prophet Ezekiel on that river plain in Babylonia. That thunderstorm was a shared experience. But what the prophet saw was something else. Ezekiel saw the glory of God, the rider of the clouds, on a sapphire throne borne along by beasts that never were, rolling on "a wheel within a wheel," an iridescent apparition come to speak with him and to put words in his mouth and send him as a prophet to his people—and that was Ezekiel's experience alone, shared by none that stood there with him. We know of it only because he put it on record, reported and recorded his unique experience.

It is doubtful that any of us has had even a comparable experience, and we accept the record as fact only if we find it credible. There is no evidence other than the report itself; in the nature of things there can be none.

Though one prophet after another reports an experience of this sort, each experience is similarly unshared, and five such visions are no more credible than is any one of them alone. That is the trouble with an unshared religious experience.

To turn now to another prophet, Jeremiah loudly said some things that panicked the authorities and they arrested him and tried him for what we might call subversion. It was a capital offense; Jeremiah had to fight for his life. When, in such a situation, this prophet had to show credentials, all he could do was to insist: "It was God who sent me; truly God sent me" (Jer. 26:12–15). He could say this and he did; but he could bring no proof—no evidence, no witnesses, simply his deposition: "God sent me." And we cannot go behind his word and verify it—or deny it either. What gave him his assurance was his unshared experience of God.

So too Amos, and Isaiah. Amos simply said: "God took me." More elaborately Isaiah said: "I heard the Lord saying 'Whom shall I send?' and I volunteered 'Here I am. Send me.' And the Lord said 'Go!' "

Call these accounts symbolic, or figures of speech, or what you will; or say that they are a man's way of putting the ineffable into words, of talking about something that you can not talk about. Leave out this imagery and say only that something happened uniquely to the prophet which was all of the authorization that he needed. We may be mystified and uneasy. We may be suspicious of visions and look around hoping for something more tangible and susceptible to verification. But that lived experience meant more for the prophet than any rational arguments or demonstrable facts. It was something primary, like seeing or hearing. He knew *because* —. Defending himself in court, Jeremiah simply said that the Lord had sent him—and his judges accepted his word, so sure was he.

There were other arguments that those prophets could have used but seemingly none of the others carried as much weight for them as this memory of an overpowering experience of God. The prophets could, and sometimes did, point to certain empirical evidence, using the pragmatic test. In the stories about the prophets their biographers pointed to the miracles those men had performed. The prophets telling their own story spoke rather of successful predictions, how they had announced in advance that Assyria would come, or the Babylonian hosts, and lay waste the land, and how events had proved them right. But this was not one of their better arguments. Not every prediction worked, and even "false" prophets turned out to be right sometimes.

A more probable source of the prophet's certainty (along with his reported experience of God) was perhaps his inability to explain his need to speak except as divine coercion. What else could compel him to speak and to act as he did?

The prophet could promptly set aside the thought that perhaps he had persuaded himself to behave as he did, his own wishes being parents to his compulsion. That was not possible, because if the prophet let himself say what he wished to say to his people, his word to them would be essentially different—false but different. The prophet was torn apart between what, as a man, he would say to his people, and what, as prophet, he *must* say. Those whom he loved he had to condemn. The tension was real and the prophet was aware of it; that painful tension may have led to his knowledge that he spoke truly. A force which he could not identify with his own human desires prompted his speech, and for him that force was "God." When it moved him he began his speech with the words "Thus saith the Lord." This voice that was not his voice he called the voice of God.

He could rule out another possibility: that his words were merely an echo of other men's words, that he was a popular preacher voicing the prevalent fancies of his public. That might be said of "false" prophets but clearly not of an Amos or Micah, an Isaiah or a Jeremiah. False prophets voiced the current moods and fashions, playing to the gallery, out to get the votes and the rewards of popularity. But the true prophet is painfully aware of the distance that separates him from his people; they make him aware of it. This prophet is the object of their hostility, the target of ridicule and violence. People did not like him because he meddled in their affairs, talked to them about how they misbehaved. Far from being an echo, the true prophet's words were an answer, a challenge, an argument. The very fact that the people could not hear the words of those prophets is the clearest proof that the prophets were not simply mouthing the popular slogans.

The prophet knew of two things that his words were not, and that knowledge left him with a certainty that they were something else. He knew that they were not what everyone else was saying, not a reflected murmur from the crowd, not his play for popularity. They had a quite different sound, so different that the people tuned the prophet out. He also knew that his words were not of his own making. They neither expressed what he wanted to say out of love and sympathy for his people, nor worked to his personal advantage and profit. Therefore he could have argued: Neither this nor that is the source of my words; neither have I invented them nor have I borrowed them from the crowd. What source suggests itself then but God? God was the postulate that explained to the prophet the prophet's need to speak. Our sophistication may suggest other options but the prophet's logic led him unerringly to God.

Also by *what* the prophet had to say for God, by its substance he knew that what he said was from his God. The prophet had his scale of values; he called some things right and precious, others wrong and tawdry. He had standards to measure his society by; justice and righteousness were his level and plumbline. And his standards were not elastic; they were fixed. The prophet knew, and the immediacy of this knowledge tied it in with God. His values, his standards, his certain knowledge were in total harmony with what the prophet knew of God. They were of God. And the prophet's need to apply to his society these values, these standards, this certain knowledge could only be God's doing. By reason of its substance this moral drive could have its source in none but God.

It is then by these four ways that the prophet knew he spoke for God: the way of the primary unshared experience which we can not prove but also not legitimately question; the empirical or pragmatic way, when events sometimes occurred as he knew in advance they must; the way of reason or logic which led him to conclude that only God could be speaking through him since surely neither his people nor his own wishes found expression in his speech—and the only source left was God; and finally, the very content of his message, which so thoroughly agreed with what to him was the nature of his God.

All of these together, or simply the first among them, the unshared religious experience, gave the prophet that measure of confidence which lent authenticity to his words and ensured their survival.

How to Be "Religious"

A DEMANDING FAITH

SOME PAGES BACK WE LEFT UNFINISHED A PROPHETIC WORD that Isaiah brought. It was in the passage where he questioned the validity of the ways men usually worship God. We let him say what religion is not; we stopped him from saying what it is. Here again is the denial, spoken as from God:

> What do your many sacrifices mean to Me?
>   God asks.
> I am fed up with the roasting rams
>   and the grease of fattened beasts . . . .
> When you present yourselves before Me
>   who wants this of you—
>   trampling My precincts? . . .
> Your newmoon ceremonies and your assemblies—
>   I hate them;
> I find them a burden;
>   they weary Me.
> When you stretch out your hands
>   I look the other way,
> And when you pray long prayers
>   I do not listen (Isa. 1:11–12, 14–15a).

This word of God according to Isaiah does not stop here. After these negations (what religion is not), a demand follows at once. And this demand is the positive, the affirmation, the program. This which follows *is* religion; this according to Isaiah is what God *does* want.

> Wash your bloodstained hands [God says];
>   be clean.
> Remove the evil of your deeds
>   from My sight.
> Cease doing wrong.
>   Learn to do good.
> Seek justice.
>   Correct oppression.
> Secure the orphan's right.
>   Take up the widow's cause (Isa. 1:15b–17).

Isaiah measured faithfulness in terms of righteousness and justice, even as justice and righteousness were the vintage which God awaited from Judah, His vineyard.

"Evil" and "oppression," like "justice" and "righteousness," are broad categories of human behavior. In theory surely most men are against the one pair of abstractions and in favor of the other. Fortunately for our understanding, Isaiah and the other prophets did not abide by generalities but said concretely what they meant. "Correct oppression," Isaiah said, and "Secure the orphan's right." Also he said "Take up the widow's cause" and (in 28:12) "Give the weary rest." He warned against specific faults. "Woe!" he said: "Woe to those that add house to house!" "Woe to them that let off the guilty in return for a bribe!" "Woe to the makers of iniquitous laws . . . framed to rob the poor of justice!" "Woe to the heroes in drinking bouts!" (5:8, 22 f.; 10:1 f.) He visited the wealthy in their homes, looked about him and said: "I see that your houses are furnished with stolen goods!" and speaking for God he asked: "What is this that you do, crushing my people and grinding the face of the poor?" (3:14f.) This was no amiable parlor talk designed to win friends and probably Isaiah was not invited again. A preacher should stick to religion.

Others among the prophets joined their voices to Isaiah's and made it wholly clear that they had a positive program to fill the gaps which their denials had made in the religious calendar. If God did not want the pomp and ceremony that went with the Temple cult, that did not mean that He made no demands. It was all a matter of place and time. Those prophets looked for religion beyond the sacred precincts: in the stores and warehouses, in the courtrooms and the legislatures, on the farms and in the households; and not alone on holy days and solemn assemblies but on ordinary weekdays as well.

Amos, Jeremiah and others agreed with Isaiah. They had questions, as we have noticed, but they also had a program—not simply questions and denials, but demands as well. Through Amos God had said:

> I despise, I reject your festive occasions,
>   and find no pleasure in your assemblies.
> When you offer Me sacrifices . . .
> And your offerings, I do not want them.
>   I turn from your gifts of fat beasts.
> Away with your choired hymns!
>   I am deaf to your instruments of song
>   (Amos 5:21-23).

Quite clearly according to Amos, this was what God does not want—but at once Amos said equally clearly what God does demand:

> Let justice roll on as waters,
>   righteousness as a steady stream (vs. 24).

Amos said it again in a climactic series of demands. First a negation: Do not.

> Do not seek out Beth-El.
> Do not visit Gilgal.
> Do not make pilgrimage to Beersheba (5:5).

Then a demand:

> Seek out the Lord, so that you may live (5:6).

Do not do that, do this. Do not seek out the shrines, seek out the Lord so that you may live. Amos is speaking riddles;

whom but the Lord do they seek when they visit their shrines? The prophet must be more specific. And so he is:

> Seek what is good and not what is evil
> so that you may live (5:14).

That is clearer: When Amos says "Seek the Lord" he means "Seek what is good." Clearer but not clear enough. What is it that is good? The next lines dissolve all doubt:

> Hate what is evil and love what is good,
> and see that justice is done in the courts (5:15).

God wants not rituals observed but justice done.

According to Jeremiah, also, God followed a denial with a demand:

> Do not rely on delusions and say: "The temple of God, the temple of God, the temple of God are these." For, only if you improve your ways and your doings—only if you promote justice between man and man, do not oppress stranger, orphan or widow . . . and do not go after other gods to your hurt, only then will I allow you to dwell in this place . . . forever and ever (7:4–7).

That is the point these prophets make; they speak, as here, of justice between man and man. What truly concerns God is how men behave towards each other. A crime against men is a sin against God but, equally, God smiles on those who serve their fellows with understanding and in love. By all means add this thought to the bleakness of the prophetic challenge reviewed in a previous chapter.

THE TWO FACES OF RELIGION

Now, although we have been limiting the field to only six among the prophets and drawing illustrations mainly from only one of these (Isaiah) we have made it all much too simple even within these limits. We may have reduced the confusion somewhat but here we need to observe that the situation is not so uncomplicated as we have made it sound. There were prophets and prophets in Bible times. The scholar (John Paterson, 1948) who called his book *The Goodly Fellowship of the Prophets* chose a misleading title. The prophets were not a goodly fellowship, not a congenial company of like-minded men, all intent on spreading the same gospel. They were much at odds with each other, and no single consistent religious position emerges from a study of their words—not something we might present as a cate-chism and call "prophetic religion"—not if we would be honest and thoughtful. In a book like Isaiah there is faith and there is faith—and faith is not always the same thing. That is why it is difficult reading. If one who is not already familiar with prophetic thought has tried reading Isaiah and has been confused, it is no cause for wonder. If he has tried reading the book and has not become confused he has probably not been reading it carefully. It speaks with more than one voice.

The second voice is not, however, what one may at first suppose; it is not the voice of "false" prophets—not here. Micah, Jeremiah, Ezekiel and others have very unkind things to say about prophets whom they call "false." Once Jeremiah refers to them with a certain generosity as misled, sincere but deluded (4:9f.), and so does Ezekiel in one very strange passage (14:9). Otherwise they appear as liars, sycophants, hypocrites, hired yes-men. Like newspapers which feature what the public wants to read, those prophets responded to popular demand, drifted with the current, blew with the wind. Such, at least, was the judgment of their canonical opposites, the name prophets. The congregation called the tune and, no doubt, the complacent, back-slapping, so-called "false" prophets "packed them in."

But when we here say: the Book of Isaiah speaks with more than one voice, we are not talking of prophets called false. In addition to the voice to which we listened in the foregoing chapter (and that was, we suggest, the authentic voice of the historical Isaiah) we can hear in the Book of Isaiah at least one other voice whose tones are genuine and whose words are equally meaningful—another voice that does not come from the chorus of the deluded.

Judaism is an amalgam—a religion made up of two sorts of faith: the kind of faith that only accepts, and the kind that requires doing. Both sorts of faith have a place in the Book of Isaiah. At times they are clearly separate; at times they stand side by side and lead us into confusion.

What does a man's religion *do* for him? It does at least two things—more perhaps but two in particular; when he is lost in doubt it gives him confidence, and when he is becalmed it beckons him on to nobler efforts. At times the face of religion is stern; at times it is gentle. Religion is a consolation, surely. It is shelter in a storm, stability in a shifting world, a source of strength in weakness, of certainty on slippery ground, of comfort in grief, of hope in sickness and despair. Religion is this, but this is not all; it is something else and different too. It is also law and authority. It deals in imperatives: "thou shalt" and "thou shalt not"; it speaks of right and wrong, of duties and responsibility; it is challenge and demand. Religion has at least these two appearances. We might call the one "comfort," the other "conscience." Religion is the source of both—the source of "ease" and of "unease"—and both are represented massively in the writings of the Hebrew prophets. In no prophetic book are these two appearances of religion so manifest and yet so confusingly intermingled as they are in the Book of Isaiah—a book not only divided down the middle to make room for a Deutero- or Second Isaiah, as has long been recognized, but also in its earlier part composed of many sorts and pieces.

But we will leave Isaiah for a while now, to take an illuminating illustration of the two types of faith from the Book of Ezekiel. Why we turn to Ezekiel will presently become clear; but first the illustration. Two passages in the Book of Ezekiel are, in the language of paradox, just nearly enough alike to be strikingly different. One is a demand; the other is a promise. In both God is speaking to Israel, speaking of "a new heart and a new spirit." The demand is in the eighteenth chapter of Ezekiel; it reads: "Cast off all of your transgressions wherewith you transgress and make yourselves a new heart and a new spirit" (vs. 31). The promise is in the thirty-sixth chapter; it reads: "I shall give you a new heart and implant a new spirit in you" (vs. 26). The result is the same: a new heart and a new spirit in God's people. It all *comes* to the same thing in the end, and yet the contrast is startling: The demand in the one: "*make* yourselves a new heart," and the promise in the other: "*I shall give* you a new heart." They are, of course, two quite different things, and the thoughts are essentially and basically opposed. In the two formulations two distinct shapes of religion confront one another and they are not to be reconciled. To be sure, an agile mind can devise a harmonizing formula. Such a formula has been proposed; it reads: "Man must strive to attain a new heart before God will bestow it." It is possible to devise such a harmonization, but it is not good to do so. The harmonizing formula introduces a meaning foreign to both passages individually, and it also reduces two colorful thoughts to one flat cliché: The Lord helps those that help themselves. Harmonizing formulas impoverish the rich religion of the prophets. It is better to recognize the diversity and to be enriched thereby.

A reader who reads each of these comparable but different sentences by itself but in its context will readily see that the contrived harmonizing formula badly warps the intention of both. The demand in Chapter 18 does not mean "You must first strive to make yourself a new heart *before* I can bestow a new heart on you"; it means "*Make yourself* a new heart." The demand is a demand, not a conditional promise. The promise in Chapter 36 does not mean "I will bestow a new heart on you *if first* you strive yourself to attain a new heart"; it means "*I will bestow* a new heart on you." The promise is a promise—also unconditional. The harmonizing formula introduces an element completely foreign to the larger meaning of the two passages as a whole. The eighteenth chapter, the one in which God demands of His people: "Make yourselves a new heart," simply has no room in it for the harmonizing thought that God will, as a matter of fact, do it Himself, Himself do all that is needed. In that eighteenth chapter not the initiative only but the doing as well is man's affair. The thirty-sixth chapter, the one in which God promises "I shall give you a new heart," this chapter simply has no room in it for the harmonizing thought that man must do his part as well. In that chapter the initiative and the doing are God's affair. In the one it is man's affair, in the other it is God's affair.

To reduce these two basic ideas to one is to lose them both. But when we regard the two ideas apart we discover, near their source, two mighty currents of religious thought, each in its purity, crystal clear, with their waters yet unmingled. Of course these currents neither began nor ended with Ezekiel. We can trace them back to still earlier generations, and we can recognize them still in our times as present expressions of two basic religious attitudes. The one is the attitude of human resourcefulness according to which a man will do for himself what he can—even to his utmost reach. The other is the attitude of human dependency, according to which a man rests in the serene faith that God will provide. Without question both of these religious attitudes find clear expression in the Bible. The better way is to recognize them—not to blur their distinctiveness, not to lose hold on their values by introducing harmonizing interpretations.

Once we accept the fact that there is diversity within the totality of the prophetic message, and decide not to be disturbed by the differences but to prize them for their distinct and separate values, we can then take the next step and consider the significance of the differences.

EACH FOR ITS SEASON

It is not that prophetic religion is ambiguous, not that God and His prophets were ambivalent, irresolute and unpredictable; they did not blow hot and cold alternately and were not stern and gentle by whim or mood. There is a meaning behind the apparent confusion, and as that meaning unfolds we will see why Ezekiel furnished our first illustration.

We spoke of the stern and of the gentler visage of religion, referred to prophetic faith as ease and as unease, as comfort and as conscience. We might recognize the presence of these two faces of religion in the prophets more readily if we called them "threat" and "promise." For the most part the prophets of Israel seem either to have threatened their wayward people with imminent destruction or to have promised their sobered nation relief and enlargement in the near or distant future.

Time and again both the threat and the promise concern Jerusalem. What the prophets said about that city's fate— now as threat, now as promise—again illustrates the contrasts and contraries to be found in the words of the prophets, the absence of any superficial harmony among them. Micah and Isaiah, Jeremiah, Uriah, and Ezekiel were among those who threatened the capital with defeat and destruction. Other prophets, Haggai and Zechariah among them, and even Ezekiel at the proper moment, promised that the ruined city would be rebuilt all glorious.

In a statement that would be long remembered, the eighth century prophet Micah gave clear expression to the threat. First he scored the leaders of Jerusalem, the princes, the priests and the prophets, for their ruthless greed and their smug confidence, and then he pictured the consequences. "Therefore," he said, "because such is your behavior, Zion shall be plowed up as a field, Jerusalem shall become ruin heaps and the Temple mount be forested heights" (3:12). That is an early classic example from the prophet Micah of the uttered threat. And this, we remember, was one of Isaiah's heresies, as well, and at about the same time.

The promise is often the precise contrary of this threat; it is the assurance that Zion will be rebuilt, the Temple restored. This is a basic and central theme when the prophetic message is hope. The prophet Zechariah phrased the promise well. He heard "good words, comforting words," he said, and the content of the words was the promise of a restored Jerusalem: "So said the Lord of Hosts: 'I am exceedingly jealous for Jerusalem and for Zion . . . I have come back to Jerusalem with compassion; My house will be rebuilt in her . . . and the [builder's] line will be stretched over Jerusalem' " (1:13f.,16). This is a promise of a rebuilt Jerusalem quite as specific as the former threat of a destroyed Jerusalem.

A reader with no knowledge of Bible history, who has observed no hints already suggesting an answer, might be inclined to ask a question such as this: What, he might ask, is the reason for this lack of decision on God's part? Why does He vacillate in this weird fashion? In one chapter in the Book of the Twelve (in Micah 3) He threatens to destroy Jerusalem; in another chapter (Zechariah 1) He is ready to build it up. Why does God not make up His mind? But a reader with only a little knowledge of the history will realize that between the one chapter and the other—between Micah and Zechariah—the Babylonians reduced the capital city to rubble, looted and burned the Temple, and carried into captivity the proud lords of Jerusalem. Micah, who threatened the disaster, lived more than a century before the event which he predicted; Zechariah, who promised restoration, lived more than half a century after that event. Two hundred years separated that threat from that promise; and not merely 200 years—the fortunes of the people were vastly different at the two ends of those two centuries. Each utterance has meaning in its setting, and there only. Threat and promise each had its setting in history, and each is complete in its independence.

Each is complete. Neither is the complement of the other; they are legitimate contraries. That is to say, Micah did not mean: as a kind of core renewal program, as a prelude to its eventual restoration, God must now destroy Jerusalem. He said what he meant. As a consequence of the social evil rampant in its midst this social structure must collapse, he said—the city and the nation will suffer destruction. That was Micah's full and complete, historically conditioned thought. Similarly Zechariah in his turn did not mean: having been destroyed simply to make way for a rebuilt city, Jerusalem now will be restored, new and beautiful. He, too, said what he meant: God is exceedingly jealous for Zion. Here and now He will provide for the rebuilding of His Temple. That is Zechariah's full and complete, historically conditioned thought.

What the two utterances have *in common* is their *difference*, the *harmony* between them is their *distinctiveness*—and this statement only sounds like double-talk. What Micah's threat and Zechariah's promise have in common is that each in turn, each in its social context, answers to a distinctive human need. The one can not do duty for the other—both would be without pertinence or meaning if we reversed their positions, the threat of ruin obviously meaningless when Jerusalem already lay in ruins, the promise of restoration similarly meaningless when Jerusalem stood haughtily invincible.

With fuzzy edges a prophetic thought is lost; only when it is seen unblurred does a prophetic word have its full value. This observation makes work for the interpreter and for the reader because the edges of prophetic sayings in the Bible are very often fuzzy—more often than not. Again and again it is as though a wash had been applied to reduce to an even grey the once positive values of a contrasting design. The task of the reader (with the necessary help of an interpreter) is to restore the original pigments, the chiaroscuro, the light and the shade.

Prophets Valid and False

PROPHETIC ANTHOLOGIES

THE READER WHO TRIES TO BRING INTO FOCUS THE TOTAL BOOK of Isaiah has a particularly difficult task. Can we approach the task of clarification by way of some figures on the length of biblical books? In a printed Hebrew Bible the Book of Isaiah may fill 93 pages, the Book of Jeremiah 107, the Book of Ezekiel 83, and the Book of the Twelve (the "Minor Prophets" from Hosea to Malachi) 81 pages. Roughly speaking, they are all pretty much the same size: 93, 107, 83, 81—all plus or minus 100 pages in a printed Bible. Probably at some time in the past these four books were written on four separate scrolls—one to a scroll. We remember that when Jesus went to a synagogue in Nazareth for a Sabbath service they handed him the Book of Isaiah that he might read the lesson (Luke 4). We remember, too, the Dead Sea Isaiah scroll complete in 54 columns of writing. Perhaps near the beginning of the Christian era the books were so written, one to a scroll. And there seems to have been a standard length—a scroll containing fifty or so columns of written text was of manageable size.

Now perhaps that explains two things. It seems first to explain the fact that material as diverse as the writings of the twelve minor prophets is included in what, according to the Jewish order, is one book—known as "the Twelve." It took that many of these smaller books to fill out the columns of a standard scroll. Secondly, it seems to explain the presence in the Book of Isaiah of the likewise diversified material which we find there. The preserved writings of the historical Isaiah were apparently enough to fill only a fraction of a standard scroll, and many other writings were added to make it a proper scroll-size scroll.

However, we must surely recognize that this observation about the standard length of scrolls explains no more than the availability of space for additional prophetic material. It says nothing whatever about how that space will be filled. No doubt, other far from mechanical factors dictated the answer to this other question. It is highly probable that, through the centuries, devoted students of the earlier prophets, constantly sensitive to the changing human needs of their new times, both searched the treasured words of their masters and, by adding current words of later prophets addressed to later problems, piously assured the ongoing contemporaneity of their prophetic source book. That was the probable course of the literary history of a book like Isaiah.

We are reaching a conclusion. We are noticing that writings of quite different sorts were combined, possibly in an almost mechanical fashion, probably according to some pattern, but combined, to make up what has come down to us as the Book of Isaiah. What would we call the Book of the Twelve if we had it as a small separate volume? I suppose we could call it a prophetic anthology—representative utterances of a dozen Hebrew prophets arranged according to authors. And what about the Book of Isaiah? Well, the fact is, that it too, properly understood, is a prophetic anthology. But there is a difference between the Book of Isaiah and the Book of the Twelve. In the Book of the Twelve the writings of the several prophets are separately identified with something like title pages—14 chapters assigned to Hosea and 14 to Zechariah, 9 chapters to Amos, 7 to Micah, 3 to Malachi, only 1 to Obadiah, and so on. Imagine the confusion if they were not identified. Imagine how strange it might seem to us to find the threat that Zion would be plowed up and Jerusalem become ruin heaps (Mic. 3:12) in the same book as the promise that God's house would be rebuilt, the builder's line stretched over Jerusalem (Zech. 1:16). These contraries are no problem as we have them—the one identified by a title page as the word of Micah (near the end of the eighth pre-Christian century), the other, in the same manner, as the word of Zechariah (near the end of the sixth), with the Babylonian conquest of Jerusalem dividing the two from each other. The title pages "unconfuse" us. But great would the confusion be if, for example, Amos simply followed on Joel with no break and no editor's title to help us. We would be as confused as—well, as we are in the Book of Isaiah. For, in the Book of Isaiah we have the same situation but with no such editorial aids. It too is a prophetic anthology—but with only one of its many prophetic authors identified by title verses. It contains writings quite as diversified as the writings collected in the Book of the Twelve and as obviously separated by centuries and events. The threat of Jerusalem's destruction and the promise of restoration alternate here as in the Twelve—and no doubt they are to be explained in the same way. In the anthology without titles which we call "Isaiah" early mingles with late and one type of religion mingles with another. Here we find the two sorts of faith and here we understand them in their historical context, each according to the human need that called it into being—*conscience* to combat arrogant complacency and languid ease, *comfort* for a people languishing in misery and paralyzed by despair.

Consider again the two quotations from Ezekiel that we used as launching pad for this excursion into literary criticism. In the one, in the demand, God said: "Cast off all your transgressions wherewith you transgress and make yourselves a new heart and a new spirit"—you must act: "*Make* yourselves a new heart." In the other, the promise, God said: "I shall give you a new heart and implant a new spirit within you"—God will act: "I shall *give* you a new heart." What is the historical context in which we can understand these two contraries? When did Ezekiel, speaking for God, make this demand and offer this promise? In all probability both of them came very soon after Jerusalem fell to the Babylonian conqueror and after the people of Judah had marched into captivity. And these two passages of demand and promise, if we understand them right, represent stages in the transition from prophetic faith of one sort to another—from the faith that requires doing to the faith that only accepts. In the despair and misery of the days following the fall of Jerusalem and the deportation of masses to Babylonia arose the human need for just such a transition. Or perhaps one should say, for just such a new emphasis. For in later Bible times and in the development of later Judaism the faith that requires doing was never wholly abandoned in favor of the other; the two flowed on side by side and their waters mingled—and we find them together still, as we have already suggested. Belief in the providence of God is such a basic element of religion that it has probably never been wholly absent. But in the despair of captivity it surely received, as Ezekiel attests, a new emphasis. Dramatically different needs demanded a dramatically different message, and Ezekiel took a decisive step. He moved from the one sort of faith to the other; the prophet became the pastor.

These observations bring us to the conclusion that the prophetic message was constantly responsive to the human need. This does not mean that these prophets were opportunists like those called "false"—shaping and reshaping their word according to the shifting moods of the populace. It means that they did not speak in a vacuum. It means that they were in touch, involved. It means that they had concern and cared.

And the God these prophets knew was not a power lofty and apart, who, having wound the world up and set it running, then looked the other way. God has concern for the fate of men. Their behavior and their condition matter to Him, and the word He sends them through His prophet is relevant to their estate. The God of the Hebrew prophets is involved in the affairs of man.

So we define more closely a thought we developed earlier. We distinguished between pastors and prophets. We did make a reservation and said we were referring to certain ones among the prophets, that we were referring to Amos, Hosea, Micah, Isaiah, Jeremiah and Ezekiel, before Jerusalem fell. The reservation was appropriate. Other prophets—those who under different circumstances brought comfort to a people in distress—among them Ezekiel, after Jerusalem fell—these may quite properly go by the name of pastors. They will find their place in our next chapter—but here a word about terminology.

WORDS OF ADMONITION AND WORDS OF CONSOLATION

Students of the prophets have recognized for centuries that these writings fall into two broad categories. They have given them different labels but always admitted their divergence. The prophet expects something bad, or he expects something good. In English, to achieve an alliteration we sometimes use the twin words "weal" and "woe" and speak of prophecies of weal and prophecies of woe. German scholars have used the contrasted rhyming terms "Heil" and "Unheil," which are German equivalents of "weal" and "woe." Anciently, the prophet Jeremiah distinguished between two types of prophets likewise according to the portent of their message. When he disputed the claims of Hananiah, he classed Hananiah with other false prophets who prophesied (here the word really means "predicted") good or peace, and he included himself in the other category, prophets who prophesied or predicted "war, disaster, and disease." "The prophets who have been of old—before you and before me," Jeremiah said to Hananiah, "prophesied for many lands and great kingdoms of war, disaster, and disease. Any prophet who prophesies good, only when what he has said comes about is it known that God has really sent that prophet" (28:7–9).

These designations focus on the *content* of the prophetic word: weal and woe; Heil and Unheil; good or peace and war, disaster or disease. It is possible to look instead at what the word does to the hearer—its purposed *effect*, as we did in the foregoing chapter. One sort of prophet may despair and communicate his desperation, foresee and threaten calamity sure to come unless his people change their way; alarmed, he may urge on his people conduct designed to avert catastrophe. As those prophets did whom we have considered, this prophet may make demands and disturb his people's peace. His threatening words may be challenging and disconcerting.

A prophet of another sort may hope with a contagious hope. He may communicate his hope to a despairing people purposing thus to revive their failing spirit. His words of promise may relieve and solace and comfort his desolate people.

Seen from the aspect of designed effect the two sorts of prophecy are best described as *challenge* and *comfort*.

It is not modern scholars alone who have noticed this difference between prophecies and prophecies. Talmudic authorities drew attention to it long ago. They wrote in Aramaic and Hebrew and they had Aramaic as well as Hebrew terms to designate the two types. Their terms are interesting enough to deserve notice.

We find matched Aramaic terms in a talmudic discussion about the order of the biblical books. This business about the order of the books is interesting in itself, showing as it does that there were then, as there are still different traditions current and different reasons adduced for the arrangement of the books. But our interest now is only in the ancient terms used for prophecies of weal and woe. The discussion is recorded in the Babylonian Talmud, in the tractate Baba Batra, 14b. An authority there explains that the biblical books of Kings, Jeremiah, Ezekiel and Isaiah are arranged in that order not for any chronological reason but to allow *calamity* to be grouped with calamity and *consolation* with consolation. The words translated "consolation" and "calamity" are old Aramaic equivalents for what we have called "weal" and "woe." The explanation makes sense only if we accept all of its premises and agree with its rabbinic author that "Kings ends with calamity, Jeremiah is all calamity which is why it follows on Kings, Ezekiel opens with calamity and ends with consolation and thus makes the transition to Isaiah, and Isaiah is all consolation." If we do not accept these unlikely premises and so reject the explanation we are still ahead. The fact remains that the talmudic authorities recognized two distinct types of prophetic utterance and gave them appropriate names: calamity and consolation.

Equivalent Hebrew terms occur in the Palestinian Talmud. A discussion there, in the tractate Berakot, V 8d, reads as follows: " . . . we find something like this among the earlier prophets, who always concluded their statements with *words of praise* and *words of consolation*. R. Eleazar objected: Except for Jeremiah who concluded with *words of admonition*. There is more to the argument but this is enough for our purpose; we have here the two contrasted Hebrew expressions, "words of consolation" and "words of admonition." Later in this same passage the words of admonition are associated with "the destruction of the Temple."

As these talmudic discussions and the distinctive terms employed unmistakably suggest, the rabbinic authorities clearly recognized the two types of prophetic discourse. In the one they found threats of punishment, predictions of calamity and specifically of the destruction of the Jerusalem sanctuary, denunciation, admonition, challenge and warning; in the other, praise and commendation, hope, comfort and consolation.

The rabbis did not, of course, create out of nothing the terms they used; the expressions had biblical roots. "Calamity" is related in content to Jeremiah's "war, disaster and disease" (28:8). "Words of admonition" recalls a statement of Amos and also something which Ezekiel said. Amos referred to any person like himself who spoke *words of reproof and admonition* in the courts of justice, saying that such a one attracted hatred to himself (5:10, cf. vs. 7). In the same manner Ezekiel refers to himself as a man given to *admonition* (3:26, cf. vs. 17). Both prophets, describing their prophetic role, use the Hebrew word for "admonish" which later the Talmud will use.

So too with the other type of prophetic literature. The rabbinic Hebrew expression "words of consolation," is a wholly adequate designation for the type of literature produced by the prophet when serving in his capacity of comforter. And this rabbinic expression, too, is descended from biblical antecedents. The opening words of the Second Isaiah, which set the tone for his own and most of the post-Exilic prophetic literature, emphatically repeat the Hebrew root which means "to comfort or console," the root which appears also in the expression "words of consolation." At the outset the Second Isaiah announces the divine charge to the spokesmen of his day: "Bring comfort, yes, bring comfort to my people" (40:1). In quite the same way and employing the same Hebrew word Zechariah conceives of the message appropriate to his times: "good words, comforting words" (1:13).

These, then, are the technical expressions in Hebrew that one might pair and adopt for use in distinguishing the two common types of prophecies: words of admonition and words of consolation—and the distinction between true and false prophets is irrelevant here. Each type of prophecy was valid, proper and legitimate in its time. And each had its time. When we considered six prophets in a previous chapter we explored the spirit of prophetic admonition. The reproving and shocking, challenging and foundation-shaking words of the eighth and seventh century prophets were wholly right in their social context. Those prophets spoke to a people prosperous and arrogant, at ease in Zion, sunning itself in the assumed indulgence of its little contractually obligated patron God. Only such words as Amos and Hosea, Micah and Isaiah, Jeremiah and the younger Ezekiel spoke had any significance in that spiritual climate.

WHEN IS A PROPHET "FALSE"?

During and after the Exile, in a totally different social setting, a now older Ezekiel and a Second Isaiah, Haggai and Zechariah, Malachi and many unnamed prophets brought to an impoverished and desperate, uprooted and remorseful populace words of consolation and encouragement, and these words of consolation were in that climate again alone significant. It is the timing that distinguishes the true from the "false" prophet. A "false" prophet speaks a good word in a wrong context. Hananiah was a false prophet. What he said, which Jeremiah contested, was that Jerusalem's God would destroy the burdensome power of Babylonia in two years' time and return to the city the Temple vessels, the king, and the captives, whom Nebuchadnezzar had carried away (Jer. 28:2-4)—a pleasant comforting word spoken at the wrong season. When the Second Isaiah says it, it is right:

> Turn aside, turn aside, depart!
>   touch no unclean thing.
> Depart in a state of purity
>   bearing the vessels of the Lord (52:11).

Spoken by Hananiah before the fall of Jerusalem, it was false.

Like Jeremiah, Ezekiel held his ground against false prophets, Jeremiah in Jerusalem, Ezekiel among the earlier captives in Babylonia, but both at the same time. In the one place as well as the other these false prophets prophesying peace were bringing a soothing but unproductive word. To those among them in reach of his voice Ezekiel said: "You have not entered the breaches and repaired the defenses about the house of Israel to enable it to withstand the battle on the day of the Lord" (13:5), and he meant: You have not filled this people's need, you have not strengthened its moral fiber, or supplied it with the resources it will require when Jerusalem falls. Ezekiel knew himself to be serving a truer purpose with his spectres of grim warning than were those distributors of rose-colored blinders. Unlike them, he was forcing his people to gaze steadily on reality and in this way preparing them to react maturely to the looming disaster.

As their opponents described them, the "false" prophets were those who in wrong circumstances always saw success ahead, who promised prosperity, who confidently said that all would be well. This is what that expression means: "They say: Peace, peace! when there is no peace"—they constantly mouth the word "peace" though peace is far from a reality (Jer. 6:14).

Here we must take care not to leave a wrong impression. Prophets who bring a comforting word are not for that reason false. They with their comforting word are "false" only if the times demand a disturbing, perspective-making word.

We are about to turn now, for the remainder of this survey, to words that could, but must not, be confused with the messages of these false prophets, words of peace designed to soothe and comfort and encourage. These words of consolation do not ring false; they are in place. Spoken against new conditions, for a society now with a wholly different mood, the words though similar have relevance and authenticity.

Ezekiel the Comforter
and Great Expectations

AROUND THE BEND

IN THE ANNALS OF HEBREW PROPHECY THE YEAR THAT JERU-
salem fell is a vantage point from which the historian of ideas
surveys the past and scans the future. There had been prepara-
tion for this moment—there were to be consequences. That
year is the great bend: behind are the prophetic words of
challenge and admonition, ahead lies the consolation.

Glancing back before turning that bend the historian can
discern in the varied landscape a dominant configuration.
With refreshing variety of form and circumstance but with
devastating monotony of theme Amos and Micah and Isaiah
in a previous century, Jeremiah and Ezekiel quite recently in
the years just before Jerusalem fell—all of these prophets—
had said in effect that Israel's God is no clucking mother bird
and that He could push His people from its comfortable nest—
that He would indeed do so. This was their essential message—up to the time when the Jerusalem Temple was reduced
to rubble.

When that had happened the prophetic message necessarily
became something quite different. When only an impoverished remnant was left in Zion, and captive Israel sat grieving

by the rivers of Babylon, Jeremiah and Ezekiel among the survivors, Jeremiah still in the environs of Jerusalem, Ezekiel in Babylonia, now spoke a prophetic word essentially new.

Look again briefly at the forebodings of the historical Isaiah and of the younger Jeremiah and Ezekiel before moving on to the new. Contrary to the fond hopes of a trusting people at ease in Zion Isaiah pictured Jerusalem's God with undeviating purpose Himself conducting the siege, giving Assyria the victory over Zion. And when, a century later, the Chaldaean battered the gates of Jerusalem, the same thought oppressed the tender prophet Jeremiah. He saw the destruction of Jerusalem as a necessary step, a final demonstration for a people suffocating in a parochial philosophy, cramped in a too narrow theology—a demonstration that their God is greater than land or people. Once and for all times, divine history was about to demolish the myth of a patron God imprisoned in a house—so said Jeremiah. Ezekiel too, Jeremiah's less sensitive contemporary, his younger counterpart in Babylonia, did not think of Jerusalem's burning and the reduction of its temple as a tragedy.

EZEKIEL

Ezekiel is the audio-visual man among the prophets, always putting on a show to draw a crowd and make a point. Watch him shave his head and beard, and with delicate scales meticulously divide the hair into three equal parts. Watch him cast one part on the fire and draw back in simulated horror as he sees it shrivel in the flame; watch him with a flashing sword wildly hack the second part; watch him on a gusty morning throw the rest into the air for the wind to carry off in all directions; then hear his application of this parable: the threefold disaster in store for the citizens of Zion—death by disease or starvation—defeat—dispersion. He had trained his people to look for meaning in everything he did; eating, weeping, his gestures, his moans—everything was grist for his sermonic mill. Even the death of his wife, the delight of his eyes, even this sorrow served him as illustration. He ostentatiously omitted the customary rites of mourning simply in order that people should be curious and ask him—and then he would tell them. When his wife died he put on the act; and when the people came as he knew they would—abominable showman that he was—he said: "I am glad you asked me. God has said: 'I am about to profane My sanctuary, the stronghold in which you take pride, the delight of your eyes . . . '" and he went on to explain that the destruction of the Jerusalem Temple would be not a tragedy but an awaited consummation (Ezek. 24:15–24). Ezekiel clearly shared the view of Jeremiah that the fall of Jerusalem was something other than a political event—that God had a hand in it, that God in fact was the effective cause.

Looking back, then, from the vantage point of Jerusalem's fall in 587—looking way back to Micah and Isaiah, or back only a few years to the still echoing words of the still vocal Jeremiah and Ezekiel—this, if one listened, is what one could hear them say: that it could happen there.

And when at last Jerusalem fell, the people understood. Ezekiel in Babylonia heard what they were saying and we have his ear-witness report of their reaction to the long predicted, now realized threat. Once, in his metaphor of national resurrection, Ezekiel repeats their doleful lament: "Our bones are dry, our hope is lost, we perish all" (37:11). And again, in a similar context of deprivation and exile, he records their remorse and dejection: "Our transgressions," they were saying, "and our sins have overtaken us; in them we waste away. How now can we live?" (33:10) It was a crisis of despair, a failure of nerve: How can we live? It was more than a military reverse, more than the defeat of their armies; they had experienced a crushing of the spirit, were bent beneath a load of self-reproach. *Self*-reproach! they had perhaps and after all, heard something of the message of their prophets. Because, of course, they might have reacted differently. They might have been totally bewildered, seeing no meaning at all in what had befallen. Or, taking another tack, they might have reproached their God, reproached Him with either of two quite unpalatable alternatives: that He had irrationally abandoned them, or that He had Himself succumbed to a superior deity—that He had showed Himself treacherous or that He had proved to be a weakling. They could have spoken so, after the fashion of those times, but Ezekiel is witness that instead they took on themselves the blame: "Our transgressions and sins have overtaken us; in them we waste away. How can we live?" Though their spirits were crushed God was still their God, and undefeated.

Who knows what might have been if Micah, Isaiah, Jeremiah, Ezekiel had not interpreted their national defeat in advance of the event, and if the exiles had not been capable of the backward look? Survival would have been questionable. Would these remnants of an uprooted people have retained their identity? Would they have survived, deprived of spiritual resources and oppressed by the thought that their God was vanquished? The fact is that the prophets had spoken and that a different explanation of their condition was ready at hand. Far from being beaten, their God had had His way; what He had planned He had accomplished. The day announced long since, the day of God according to Amos— the day of cloud and thick darkness according to Ezekiel— that day had come. But prophets had pointed the way to survival, and it led not away from a defeated God but towards a God who cares. History had meaning.

That backward look was one factor making for survival. The new prophetic message was another. Jeremiah and Ezekiel lived to achieve a transition. The times of Ezekiel gave birth to the pastoral ministry and to the prophetic words of consolation. With a large assist from Jeremiah and impelled by the crisis of those perilous times Ezekiel became

a pastor—a shepherd of sheep, concerned for persons as well
as people.

THE EMERGENCE OF THE INDIVIDUAL

Jeremiah had set a kind of pattern for Ezekiel with his
promises to certain men of good will. God had authorized
Jeremiah to promise survival to his devoted disciple Baruch,
and to the Ethiopian Eved-melech. So to the one—to Baruch
—Jeremiah said:

> I will bring disaster down upon all flesh,
> God says, but I will give you your life as
> reward wherever you go (45:5).

To the other, to Eved-melech who had saved Jeremiah from
death in the dungeon, the prophet said:

> I am carrying out My word against this city,
> for ill and not for good . . . but I will
> rescue you on that day, God says . . . ; your
> life will be your reward—because you
> trusted Me (39:16–18).

Because survival had meaning for Jeremiah, again when
Jerusalem was under siege he used the phrase "your life as
reward."

> So God has said: I offer a way of life and a
> way of death: Whoever remains in this city
> will die by the sword, by famine, or by
> disease. But whoever goes, and surrenders to
> the Chaldaeans who are attacking you, will
> live and his life will be his reward (21:8f.).

These too would have their lives as reward, he said—the
defenders of the city who had the perspective to know what
must befall and who, exercising their human prerogative,

made the proper choice—these would have their lives as reward. It was with the promise of life that Jeremiah rewarded also the loyal Rechabites (35:19).

Here we have it then—the beginning of that concept of the saved remnant—here and not in the Isaiah of an earlier century. Because of their superior merit these few will survive the unitary national disaster—this according to the teaching of Jeremiah.

Here too we have, in the repeated appeal to life as reward, an early example of the Jew's fierce will to live—the value he puts on life.

And here, finally, we have the thought which led Ezekiel to his pastoral activity. In this repeated pattern in Jeremiah one sees the individual emerging from the mass and rating, according to this prophet, God's person to person attention.

Developing the pattern set by Jeremiah, Ezekiel proposes a first somewhat tentative answer to the people's despair. When Ezekiel heard them give way to hopelessness and ask "How can we live?" he answered their one question with three of his own. "Why should you die?" he asked (33:11), and he quoted God's questions as he had heard them: "Do I at all wish the death of the wicked? Do I not rather wish that he should turn from his way and live?" (18:23) The questions add up to a statement. God too is on the side of life.

This thought is developed in Ezekiel's eighteenth chapter, the chapter in which the prophet denies the validity of the current saying: "The fathers ate sour grapes and the teeth of the children are on edge." No, God says through Ezekiel: "All persons are in My hand, the father as well as the son. The wicked is the one who dies" (vs. 4). With such reasoning this prophet means to free the individual from the shackling force that we call "cultural determinism." The prophet both gives and takes. He does indeed relieve the individual of the sense of being caught up in the sticky mass, but at the same time he deprives him of his excuses and alibis; a man should not blame society for what he is, he stands on his own feet. Not only that, he also is capable of choices; he is what he becomes. "When a wicked man turns from his wickedness and does what is right, he saves his life" (18:27). So—make yourselves a new heart. . . .

As far as it went this argument of Ezekiel was a beautiful answer to the despairing question of the guilt-laden exiles. It was pragmatically right, a lifting of burdens, an antidote against lethargy, a brace for weak knees. It was a first shape of hope.

Ezekiel had yet other answers—answers that run the whole gamut from human to divine resources. We noted a polarity between the demand: "Cast off all of your transgressions wherewith you transgress and make yourselves a new heart and a new spirit" (18:31)—the polarity between this demand and the divine promise: "I shall give you a new heart and implant a new spirit within you" (36:26). Ezekiel paces the steps between the one pole and the other, the gamut of hope. But so do other prophetic personalities who have contributed anonymously to the prophetic anthology known as the Book of Isaiah. Instead of staying with Ezekiel for examples of consolation, consider now those chapters in Isaiah which quite clearly draw several shapes of hope guaranteed by God—hope that God fulfills, hope that requires no human effort.

"MESSIAH"

One of these divinely promised boons goes by the name of "messianic" hope. In later religious development this one among the shapes of hope attained the most significance and it here asks for the most attention.

Approaching this hope we at once become involved with technical things—with languages and grammar: with adjectives, and nouns, and verbs, and participles, and Greek, and Hebrew, and such. "Messianic" is an adjective related to the noun, "messiah," and messiah is the English spelling of an old Hebrew participle pronounced *mashiach*. Hebrew, of course, is the language of the Hebrew Scriptures, the language David spoke and Isaiah and Elijah and all the Jewish people of their times. Later, in the time of Jesus and Paul, in the New Testament times, Jews spoke other languages as well. When Jesus calls God "Abba" he is using the word for "Father" in a language called Aramaic, the language of parts of the Bible (especially Daniel) and a large part of the Talmud. The New Testament as a whole was written in Greek. Those were the three languages used by Jews in the time of Jesus: Hebrew, Aramaic and Greek.

Now to get back to grammar: Old Hebrew has a verb *mashach* which means "to anoint," "to pour or rub oil or ointment on a person or thing." Anointing served various purposes. Soldiers anointed their shields to keep the thick leather from drying and cracking. Men and women anointed their bodies with oil for cleansing and care. But that feature of anointing that is related to hope is its ceremonial use as a symbol imparting holiness to a utensil or garment or person. The Pentateuch contains an example. After the skilled artisans had made the wilderness ark and tabernacle, the altar and its utensils, the garments and ornaments of the priests, Moses anointed these objects with a prepared ointment and this was intended to make them holy or separate, to set them aside for a sacred purpose (Lev. 8:10f.).

So it was with things. The Hebrews also used anointing to lend distinction to persons in biblical times. A survey suggests that ancient Israel anointed men to leadership; in the earlier times they anointed kings, in later biblical times they anointed priests. And the act of pouring or rubbing the special, perfumed ointment on the heads of these persons conferred holiness, so they thought. Anointing was a symbol of separation for a sacred purpose. One could describe the priest or king, who had been set apart by this ceremony, simply by calling him "the anointed one," in Hebrew *ha-*

mashiach, "the anointed," and the context would tell whether he was king or priest: the *mashiach* was "the king" or "the priest," as the case might be.

To get back to grammar and languages: just as the verb "to anoint" yields in English a passive participle "[one who is] anointed," so in Hebrew the verb *mashach* yields *mashiach*, with the same meaning. But, as we have noted, the word *mashiach* is simply the sound in the original Hebrew of the familiar English noun "messiah" (*mashiach*—messiah), from which we derive the adjective "messianic," which originally meant "related to the anointed one, to the messiah, the king."

The men who translated the Bible into Greek, a couple of centuries before the Christian era, consistently translated the Hebrew verb *mashach* with forms of the Greek verb *chriein*. When they came to the passive participle *ha-mashiach*, "the messiah," "the anointed," they consistently translated it *ho christos* and this is easily recognized as the original pronunciation of the word which in English we pronounce "the Christ." A follower of *ho christos* is a Christian. So here we have an equation: The Hebrew word *ha-mashiach*, pronounced in English "the messiah," is the word which the Greek-speaking Jews translated *ho christos*, pronounced in English "the Christ," and all of these words originally meant "the anointed one," the anointed priest, or according to the context, "the anointed king."

MONARCHIC EXPECTATIONS

Enough now of grammar and language. One of the two types of persons who were anciently anointed has special interest in this context of comfort. If one were asked to name a person in the Hebrew Bible who was anointed, one would probably think first either of Saul or of David. And that would be quite natural. The story of the prophet Samuel anointing the young Saul, who had gone in search of his father's asses, is one of the most dramatic in the Bible. A young man goes on a simple errand and finds a kingdom. Well known too is the story of Samuel's later rejection of Saul in favor of David whom he anointed in turn. It will also be remembered that David had his own son Solomon anointed to succeed him, and that at the division of the kingdom Solomon's son Rehoboam followed him to the throne of Judah. From that time onward during the entire history of that southern kingdom Judah, that is to say, for four hundred years or more, a descendant of David by way of Solomon and Rehoboam occupied the throne of Judah in the capital city Jerusalem. Except for one insignificant interval of five or six years when a queen ruled the land the Davidic line was unbroken from 1004 to 587 B.C.E. At the close of this long period Zedekiah was taken captive to Babylonia. Zedekiah's defeat meant tragedy. When he was captured he was not simply killed, or simply carried away as a captive to an alien land. He was plundered. The great king his captor, Nebuchadnezzar, took his sight from him. But before he put out Zedekiah's eyes he gave him a memory. The last that Zedekiah saw was the slaughter of his children, the child princes, his hope. Then he descended into a life of darkness (II Kings 25:6f.).

If there had been no collateral line the execution of these princes would have meant the end of the royal Davidic dynasty. But as it happens, the son of Zedekiah's older brother was already a prisoner in Babylonia and he was not killed when Zedekiah was taken captive. This nephew, Jeconiah, had been king before his uncle. (His royal name Jehoiachin is more familiar.) This younger man survived the fall of Jerusalem, being safer in his prison in Babylonia than his cousins were in the royal palace in Jerusalem. The deposed and captive king Jehoiachin had sons, and a grandson. Without doubt his grandson was born in Babylonian captivity; he bore a Babylonian name—Zerubbabel. We shall want to look at him again.

But first a parallel, an observation, and a question. The parallel: For nearly two centuries now the United States of America has been a democracy. We cannot think of America as anything other than a democracy. When Babylonia invaded and conquered the kingdom of Judah in 587, for more than four centuries that little state had been a kingdom. It had never been anything other than a kingdom, a monarchy, and no one could think of it except as such.

The observation: Since the time when Samuel anointed David, before the year 1000 B.C.E., in Jerusalem the word "king" meant an anointed descendant of David. No one could think of a king in Jerusalem without thinking of the dynasty of David. A Judean king simply meant an anointed descendant of David.

And now the question: What would pass through the minds of the Jews in Babylonian captivity when they considered the possibility of rebuilding their state? That possibility dawned, of course. When the Jewish captivity had gone on for fifty years Cyrus the Persian conquered Babylon and decreed that the Jewish captives there, mostly no doubt the second or third generation of those whom Nebuchadnezzar had deported—Cyrus decreed that they might return to Jerusalem and rebuild it, might take with them the vessels brought as loot from the Temple there, and so restore the Temple building and its worship (Ezra 1). In his decree Cyrus said nothing about statehood for the people who would return and restore the Temple and the city on Mount Zion; but what must have passed through the minds of those people as they prepared for the trip to the home of their fathers? Not what passed, appropriately, through the minds of Jews in recent years in Palestine when they prepared to reconstitute the state of Israel—not that they would be a constitutional republic. If in time they were to be a state again, independent of Persia and self-determined, it followed as a matter of course in those ancient days that the state would be a kingdom and also as a matter of course, that an anointed descendant of David would sit on the restored throne of the kingdom.

Matters took their course. Another twenty years passed before very many people from Babylonia, now under Persian rule, had joined those Jews who never had left the environs of Jerusalem. Time passed before prophets like Haggai and Zechariah had aroused enough enthusiasm among the population to get them to undertake the work of rebuilding; but after a while the Temple was in fact ready—the Temple and something else. The sources are somewhat inadequate but a number of plausible inferences suggest that this is what happened: While the Second Temple was building, a party in Jerusalem was hoping for something more than the restoration of the worship service there. This group was indeed hoping for independence from Persia, hoping that Judah might again become an independent state. Remembering that statehood meant a monarchy, and that a king of Judah was always an anointed descendant of David, what then could statehood mean but the restoration of the monarchy with a branch of the tree of Jesse enthroned in Jerusalem—a descendant of Jesse the father of David. Such a branch, or twig, or shoot from the royal family tree, was, of course, available. He was in Jerusalem and, encouraged by Haggai and Zechariah, he had taken a leading part in the project of rebuilding the Temple. He was the grandson of Zedekiah's nephew, the grandson of Jeconiah or Jehoiachin, as we have seen: the princely Zerubbabel.

A DISAPPOINTED HOPE

There was only one trouble. Apparently Cyrus's failure to mention independent statehood for Judah in his decree, which simply permitted the people to go home and rebuild their Temple—apparently his failure to mention independence was not an oversight. Persia had no intention of letting Judah go. And the Temple was rebuilt and dedicated, and the little community in and around Jerusalem got on quite well—but as a province of the Persian empire, not as a self-determined, self-governing state—no kingdom, no Davidic king, none crowned or anointed, no *mashiach*. We do not know what happened to Zerubbabel. There is only a single enticing and puzzling bit of information to the effect that a crown made-to-measure for Zerubbabel was in fact stored up as a souvenir in the Temple treasury—a souvenir only, a monument to a beautiful dream (Zech. 6:14).

But old visions do not die. They experience sublimation. And the wish for a king, for the restoration of the monarchy, the wish that proved politically unfeasible, was not abandoned, it was transplanted—moved from the field of politics to the fertile soil of religion.

It is not known that this was the origin of the messianic hope which Judaism and Christianity share, but most probably it was. In all likelihood it grew out of the frustrated attempt to constitute Judah an independent state and to anoint a descendant of David in the person of the prince Zerubbabel, to occupy the throne in Jerusalem. An unsuccessful political maneuver became a long-term captivating ideal.

Other Shapes of Hope

A MESSIANIC KING

To be sure, the hope for a king and what we think of when we speak of the messianic hope are not identical. The political ambition and the religious ideal are not the same thing. The one went through a proper transformation before it became the other. Three things happened, in the thought of the prophets.

One: *God took the initiative.* That is to say: Prophets taught the view that there would be a messianic king only when God was ready. Not a military coup to seat a candidate, not any human strategy, would bring on the day. It would be God's willing and doing. Expressed in terms that are now familiar, the hope for a king was transferred from the area of the faith that required doing to the area of the faith that only accepts. It was a pretty general reorientation; several shapes of hope belong to this latter area of faith, among them the messianic ideal. As far as the biblical evidence goes and disregarding later developments, there is not much that men are called on to do to forward that ideal. They are merely encouraged to believe in and to hope for the time of its fulfillment.

The second thing that happened is that *the king was idealized:* the prophets and people associated the noblest of human virtues with the envisioned person of the king. He would indeed be charismatic, that is to say, more than commonly gifted. On this future ideal king God's spirit would rest, a spirit of wisdom and discernment, of counsel and strength, of knowledge of God and fear of God. He would be gifted too with more than common human intuition; he would be able to see what is not on the surface and to hear the unsaid. He would exercise justice and that would be the stability of his reign. "He will judge the poor in righteousness," one passage says, "and decide with equity for the lowly of the land." The scabbard and the holster at his waist would house not a sword and pistol but righteousness and justice. The peace he would bring would be unending, his reign perpetual. This king could be called "Wondrous Counselor, God-like Hero, Father Forever, Prince of Peace."

And this too happened (in the third place): *the king ideal was universalized*. It would not be Judah alone, prophets said, that would enjoy the security, the peace, the stability, which his reign would bring, but all nature would be regenerate, the jungle would be tamed, and the earth would be filled with the knowledge of God as the ocean bed with its waters.

The two passages that contain the most specific references to the ardently awaited messianic king appear in the ninth and eleventh chapters of Isaiah. Not every scholar will agree, but it is highly probable that these passages were written after the disappearance of Zerubbabel, at least two centuries after the time of the Isaiah who gave his name to the book. They are included in the prophetic anthology which is called Isaiah but they are not by that Isaiah. They must be dated not at the end of the eighth century, when Isaiah lived, but in the fifth pre-Christian century or later.

Read these passages and watch for the three features just mentioned: (1) that God takes the initiative and *gives* to mankind His messianic king, (2) that the king, though a shoot of the tree of Jesse, is *idealized*—and especially as concerns his moral nature, and (3) that the ideal is *universalized*, for the benefit of all mankind, all nature.

These three features all appear in the passage in the eleventh chapter of Isaiah:

A shoot will come forth from the root-stock of Jesse,
    from his roots a sprout will grow
And the spirit of the Lord will rest on him,
    the spirit of wisdom and discernment,
The spirit of counsel and strength,
    the spirit of knowledge and fear of the Lord.
Not by what is openly apparent will he judge,
    nor will he decide by what his ears have heard;
He will judge the poor in righteousness
    and decide with equity for the lowly of the land,
And he will rebuke the land with the rod of his mouth
[Instead of *land* a plausible conjecture would read *tyrant*.
    And he will rebuke the tyrant with the rod of his mouth],
    and fell the wicked with his lips' breath.
His waist will be girt with righteousness
    and faithfulness will be the girdle of his loins.
Then the wolf will dwell with the sheep
    and the leopard will lie down with the kid
And the calf and the lion will feed together
    and a young lad will be able to lead them.
And the cow and the bear will pasture together;
    [together] their young will lie down,
    and the lion will feed on hay like the cattle.
And the infant will play by the den of the asp,
    and the [just] weaned child will put his hand over
                the adder's nest.
Men will not work harm or destruction
    in all of My holy mountain,
For the earth will be filled with the knowledge
              of the Lord
    as is the ocean bed with its waters.

Also in Isaiah 9 the three new features appear—divine initiative, idealized ruler, universal sway:

The people wandering in darkness
    will see a great light;

For them that inhabit a land of deep darkness
    light will yet dawn.
You will increase their joy
[God must be addressed here—You, O God, will],
    multiply their happiness.
They will rejoice in Your presence
    as at the joy of the harvest,
    as men rejoice dividing the spoil.
For the burdensome yoke that they bear,
    the rod laid about their shoulders
And their taskmasters' whip
    You will break as when You defeated Midian.
Yes, every army boot noisily tramping,
    every uniform rolled in gore
Will be burnt,
    be fed to the flames.
Because a child will be brought forth,
    we will have a son
And he will be clothed with authority
    and bear the name:
Wondrous Counselor, God-like Hero,
    Father Forever, Prince of Peace.
He will exercise complete authority
    and peace will be limitless
On the throne of David
    and throughout his kingdom
To establish and to sustain it
    in justice and righteousness,
From now on and forever.
    The zeal of the Lord of Hosts will accomplish this.

Here then is the dream, now given a moral purpose and
universalized, advanced to a gleaming hope and entrusted to
God for His power and His will to realize. According to the
faith that only accepts, "the zeal of the Lord of Hosts will
accomplish this."

There are other passages than these two in Isaiah express-
ing the hope for a messiah, for a king divinely endowed and

destined to introduce peace on earth, but not as many such passages as one might suppose. Material properly called "messianic" is indeed historically significant but its bulk is by no means extensive. Predicting the coming of a future king, a Davidic messiah, was far from a major preoccupation of the Hebrew prophets. Much has grown out of little.

THE KINGDOM OF GOD

What we call "messianic" is not, however, exhausted by the passages which refer to the Davidic messiah, because we stretch the meaning of the word and include under the same heading another significant shape of hope. It might seem here that we are stretching the word a bit far; we are about to call by that name a form of hope that is messianic but without a messiah, without a Davidic king. And yet to do so is justifiable because, for one thing, except for the person of the human king it *is* the same hope. It is a hope for universal peace on earth, the end of war, the taming of the wild, a society of just and righteous men enjoying the bounties of this earth. It is quite the same result though the way to the goal is somewhat different. It is still God's doing; it still belongs in the area of the faith that only accepts. But this shape of messianic hope is a hope for God's *direct* entry into the affairs of men. It is not that He will *send* a king of David's line: He will *come* as king; God will Himself be king. This hope is for the coming of God's kingdom, the kingdom of God on this earth. We do not, of course, *have* to call this hope messianic, though commonly we do. A suitable term perhaps would be "the Utopian ideal," but better still the familiar "Messianic Age." Several passages in Isaiah give expression to the messianic ideal in this form—two in particular. In the fifty-first chapter of Isaiah God summons His people to hear His announced intent:

> Listen to Me, My people,
>> hearken to Me, My folk.
> For revelation proceeds from Me
>> and I set in motion My truth to serve as a
>>> light for the nations.
> About to be fulfilled is My sure purpose, My
>> salvation has gone forth;
> and My arms will arbitrate among nations.
> The coastlands put their hope in Me;
>> for My arm they wait (vs. 4f.).

The classic prophetic formulation of this messianic ideal appears twice in prophetic literature, once at the beginning of the second chapter of Isaiah and again in the fourth chapter of Micah. Probably neither of these name prophets was its author; apparently the historical Isaiah and the historical Micah lived several hundred years too soon to have formulated this hope. But no matter! Whether it was one of these men or someone else whose name we do not know, the author of this passage was one of the great spirits of the past and his words had formative influence on our culture and our ideals. Here we quote the passage as it appears in Micah 4 because there it includes a meaningful thought now missing from the parallel in Isaiah. It is almost too familiar to need quoting, but read it again and watch for two features: for the ethical in it and for the universal. Watch also for the two promised "freedoms": the freedom from fear and the freedom from want.

> At the end of days
>> the mountain of the Lord's house
> Will be established as the highest mountain
>> and be lifted above the hills.
> Then nations will flow to it,
>> many peoples will go and say:
> "Let us go up to the mountain of the Lord,
>> to the house of the God of Jacob,

That He may reveal His ways to us
  and that we may follow in His paths."
For revelation will come from Zion,
  the Lord's word from Jerusalem.
And he will arbitrate among great peoples,
  set aright distant populous nations.
Then they will beat their swords into plowshares
  and their spears into pruning hooks,
And people will not raise sword against people
  and will learn war no more.
They will sit every man under his vine
  and under his fig tree, with none to make them afraid—
For the Lord of Hosts has spoken.

For our world in these days this ancient glorious ideal has special pertinence. It is the focus of our dreams, our one greatest hope.

AGAIN "THE DAY OF THE LORD"

Not all the shapes of biblical hope are equally attractive. Consider only two more among the several that remain. The key word for the one is "Armageddon," for the other "Apocalypse." Both are aspects of, or developments out of, the old idea of the coming great day of the Lord. That was the cherished popular notion which, as we remember, Amos undertook to explode, when he asked: "What is your interest in the day of the Lord?" and said "It will be darkness and not light" (5:18). Speaking so, Amos was rejecting the hope in a day to come, awesome and final, a day which would strike with calamitous defeat all the armies of all the nations that ever waged war against Zion; God, the people thought, would be victorious on that day, and His people triumphant. This popular expectation the prophet Amos could not share. But if the challenge of Amos and Isaiah and others dampened the spirits of those who then hoped for that day, and if events at the time of Assyria's conquest of the Northern

Kingdom and Babylonia's victory over Judah could be regarded as the fulfillment of the evil forebodings of those earlier prophets, if indeed the day of Jerusalem's fall was, as Ezekiel could call it, "a day of cloud and deep darkness" (34:12), even these grim realities could not erase the dream. Speaking of the hope for a king we said: "Old visions do not die; they experience sublimation." As it was with the desire for a king, after the Zerubbabel failure, so it was with the longing for the day of the Lord. Late in Bible times—we cannot say just when—it experienced a rebirth—as twins.

"ARMAGEDDON"

We name one of these twins "Armageddon," a name which occurs in the Book of Revelation, the last book of the New Testament. Mentioned there is "a place which is called in Hebrew 'Armageddon'" (Rev. 16:14,16). Since it is said to be a Hebrew name we should recognize it, but since the name nowhere occurs in Hebrew we must fall back on the usual guess at its meaning. Put the Greek letters into Hebrew letters and the place sounds like *har megiddo* which means the mountain of Megiddo. We know where Megiddo is, but, to our confusion, it is a city in a plain—on a built up mound, to be sure, but in a plain—in the north of Canaan. It is a mound but no mountain, a *tell* but no *har*. When its site is mentioned in the Hebrew Bible, reference is made to "the waters of Megiddo" (Judg. 5:19) or to "the plain of Megiddo" (II Chron. 35:22) and once even more clearly to the plain of Megiddo*n*, but never to the mountain of Megiddo. The waters, or the plain of Megiddo*n* with a final *n* as in Armageddon (Zech. 12:11), are an ancient battleground of nations, and because such a battle of nations is what is involved in the New Testament reference it is customary to overlook the "mountain" part of the name and to take Armageddon simply as a symbol for a place of mortal international conflict, as a symbol for the last, the ultimate war. At any rate it has come to be used in that sense; it stands for the calamitous battle at the end of days when, as we read in Joel 4:10, reversing the Utopian process, men will assemble vast arsenals, beating their plowshares into swords and their pruning hooks into spears, when nation *will* again raise sword against nation and fight the final suicidal fight, the war to end all wars, the thermonuclear holocaust which none will survive.

Here, of course, the thought is rephrased in modern idiom, and one detail has also been omitted. According to the biblical view there *would* be survivors on that terrible day of the Lord, not many but some survivors, and that makes of the expectation, grim though it surely is, a shape of hope. In the final day of the Lord some would survive—his elect; there lies the hope.

Two or three passages will be enough to illustrate also this not too elevating concept, and again two are from the Book of Isaiah though they are hardly in the spirit of the eighth century prophet. In the first passage the people of Jerusalem appear to be speaking: God is "with" them.

> Be broken, O nations, and dismayed,
>   and hearken you ends of the earth.
> Gird yourselves and be broken,
>   gird yourselves and be broken;
> Take counsel together but it will be frustrated,
>   say your word but it will not prevail,
>   for God is with us (Isa. 8:9f.).

"God is with us"—there is the hope in this grim expectation. In the other passage a prophet is speaking:

> As a starving man dreams that he is eating,
>   and awakens with his hunger unsatisfied,
> As a thirsty man dreams he is drinking,
>   and awakens and is faint with his thirst unslaked.
> So will the swarm of nations be
>   that lay siege to Mt. Zion (Isa. 29:8).

Or, as in another verse in the same chapter:

> The swarm of your foes will be [blown
>   away] like fine dust,
>   the swarm of tyrants like driven chaff (vs. 5).

Again it is the foes of Zion that fall; Zion survives.

But the best illustration of this thought is found in another biblical book—in two of the later chapters of the Book of Ezekiel, in the vision there of the destruction of the mighty hosts of Gog, king of the probably mythical land of Magog. (Magog is a land, not a person; it is Gog *of* Magog.) The story is too long, and perhaps too repulsive as well, to justify our quoting it here. One may want to read it in Ezekiel 38 and 39—but not for pleasure—except of course that "we" survive.

APOCALYPSE

Finally, now, some thoughts on apocalypse, the second of the twins. "Apocalypse" means a revealing (of the hidden). What apocalypse purports to reveal is the distant future— what will happen at the end of time. The future, of course, is hidden. Unless He consents to reveal it through His chosen instruments God alone knows the future. When He does so reveal it we have apocalypse.

In English we say the future lies ahead—our past is behind us. Not so in Hebrew. In Hebrew, words that refer to time past, *temol, kedem, lefanim*, are spatially ahead of us, before us, out in front where we can see them; and properly so. The past has already been revealed, is visible. It is the invisible future which lies behind us, where we have no eyes. The future is *'acharit*, the end of time is *'acharit hayamim*, "the days back there," and properly so. The future has yet to be revealed. A glimpse into the future "back there" is apocalypse.

If we can speak of hope in such terms, the apocalyptic hope is terrifying—a terrifying hope. It is only by a certain courtesy that we can speak of it as hope at all. It is hopeful if we assume development within the vision, episodes, the last of which is blessing. Stark terror is the apocalyptic mood; but it yields in the end to peace. Worlds crash and splinter. The wobbling earth grows dizzy, overturns and spills its load of corruption. But *these* somehow stay. In the calm that ensues they are there—the blessed.

The thread is hard to follow but there is a kind of story. It resembles Noah's flood. In the dim past primeval creation had grown stale. God saw and resolved to flush clean His corrupted earth. He submerged all rotting flesh, but He was both provident and discriminating. He closed the vessel's hatch upon one man and his wife and household. The upright Noah survived to hear God's rainbow promise. That story of the flood in primeval days serves as pattern for the apocalypse at the end of days.

But the story is only the frame and the conception is cosmic. The prophet who wrote the chapters 24 to 27 of Isaiah foresaw a day of fierce and universal judgment:

> On that day God will punish
>   the heavenly hosts in heaven
>   and the earthly kings on earth . . .
> And the moon will be abashed and the sun ashamed,
>   for the Lord of Hosts will reign
> On Mount Zion; in Jerusalem,
>   and before His elders will His glory be (24:21, 23).

The powerful accents and the crashing sounds of the Hebrew original are muted in translation but the mad dance is yet revealed.

> Lo, God will empty and ravish the earth,
>   turn it over and scatter its inhabitants. . . .
> Terror and pit and snare
>   are about you, who inhabit the earth.

> He who runs from the noise of the terror
>   shall tumble into the pit;
> He who scrambles from the pit
>   shall be caught in the snare. . . .
> Utterly broken the earth,
>   utterly shattered the earth,
>   dizzily tottering the earth,
> Drunkenly the earth reels,
>   sways like a hammock. . . . (24:1, 17–18a,
>   19–20a).

Almost, the author of this passage sees the world revert to the chaos before the beginning.

In the word "almost" lies the hope. Noah escaped the all-destroying deluge because his goodness had won God's favor. Similarly in the apocalyptic vision a certain few escape the universal catastrophe, but the author of the vision is far from explicit as to why they do. Possibly he excepted them also from the general condemnation—silently implied that they were not among the defilers of the earth. Whatever the rationale the hope is real. Those elect, whom God here calls "My people," will survive though the heavens collapse—this remnant will survive and see the dawn of a never-ending day—paradise regained (26:20).

Apocalypse is the answer when there is no answer. On defeat desperation fathers apocalypse. At the end of his resources, man expects no help, no salvation short of a violent invasion by the supernatural into human history. This invasion is apocalypse. That it takes weird forms in the frantic mind is not surprising. What awakens our wonder is this: that the author of apocalypse is capable of retaining a balanced sense of right. Apocalypse is ethically motivated: not any whim, demonic or divine, is the cause of the cataclysm, but the unbounded transgression of the earth's inhabitants. And also this: that, with a faith which looks beyond the visible, the author of apocalypse can say to God:

You keep in perfect peace the spirit of him
who trusts,
if in You he trusts.

And that he can counsel man:

Trust in God forever,
for God is a rock of ages (26:3 f.).

A Job to Do—a Mission

THERE ARE TWO KINDS OF HOPING. MEN CAN HOPE WITH A SERENE and perfect faith, and simply wait supine and open-mouthed for the realization of all desires. Apocalypse and messianism have served as illustrations for this first kind of hoping. But men can also hope with a determined hope, and move with a sure tread towards a desired goal. We turn now to this kind of hoping—and our key word is "mission."

If I am sent to do a job I am given a mission. If I have been given a job to do I have become a missionary. A people with a job to do is a missionary people. A religion that includes a mission is a missionary faith.

In a block of sixteen chapters in the Book of Isaiah, and in another interesting little book called Jonah, we find the best examples of those features of prophetic thought which we associate with the idea of a mission.

THE SECOND ISAIAH

The block of chapters is the sixteen that begin with Isaiah 40 and extend through Isaiah 55. The author of these chapters held out to the Judean captives the hope that Cyrus the Persian would break the power of Babylonia and send those captives home. Centuries ago it was recognized that the author of these sixteen chapters was not the prophet Isaiah who lived in the eighth pre-Christian century and threatened Jerusalem with destruction at the hands of Assyria. The author of the sixteen chapters lived no less than two-and-a-half centuries later than that first Isaiah, and under a wholly different political constellation; also, he lived not where the first Isaiah lived, not in Jerusalem, but in Babylonia. He is not the same person; we know very little about him; we do not even know his name. For convenience we call him the "Second" Isaiah—by which we simply mean Chapters 40–55 of the Book of Isaiah. And we call him "Isaiah" simply because his writings were included in the Isaiah scroll.

What this so-called Second Isaiah said to his people was, like all genuine prophetic words, relevant to the then current human situation. As with other prophets this one did not speak in a vacuum; he brought a word of God which answered to a people's present need. The people of Israel were in need of comfort and he comforted them; they were as refuse and he came to rehabilitate them. And what better way to rehabilitate persons or a people than to provide them with a worthy goal, a purpose for their life, a job to do! This was the time for a mission and it was probably the prophet whom we call the Second Isaiah who conceived and propagated the idea of Israel's mission. It seems to have sprung from the historical context of his place and time.

THE MEANING OF "MISSION" AND "SALVATION"

Persons can use the same words in a conversation and woefully fail to communicate, talking right past each other. This is particularly true of theological terms, and all readers may not mean the same thing when they use words like "mission" —or like "salvation," which also we will refer to in this context. It may be well therefore to clarify the meaning of these two words before we go on, so that we may not seem to be thinking of quite different concepts, and may doubt that we should be calling them "mission" and "salvation" at all. When we are dealing with the thinking of the Hebrew prophets it is proper to use these words as we will. We will use them with the meaning the words had in the days of those prophets; what other meanings they have now have been added since the time of the prophets in a culture predominantly Christian.

When the Second Isaiah sent his people on a mission he sent them to give to all men a religion to live by. His people's goal was a reconciled humanity. Their mission was to the society of men for its earthly good. Their interest was in the quality of men's lives here and now, and in the kind of world they could leave for their children's children. They were not interested in the fate of their own souls in an afterlife. They did not think of achieving heavenly bliss or escaping the torments of hell. They did not think of such matters because the time had not yet come when Jews thought in those terms. The fate of men's souls in an afterlife did not occupy a place in the thought of biblical man. He had this life to live; he did not know anything about life after death and made no provision for it.

We speak here of what did *not* concern men in the time of the prophets in order to make more obvious by comparison what *did* concern them. The term "salvation" as, for example, the Second Isaiah used the term, had none of the associations with eternity which have subsequently gathered round it. In the Bible salvation is not a second chance at life. This is a man's life; and if it is lived in hunger and misery and hurt, in anxiety and servitude and lonely grief, it may be only a fragment of a life—one may not call it living—but this is it. There is no life to save but this life, and salvation is in essence the rescue of the huddled masses from present terror and want.

The Hebrew nouns which mean "salvation" are all derived from a verb which means "to help, to save or deliver." Often, according to the context, the verb means no more than "to deliver persons or armies, cities or nations from danger," from an enemy or from any other threat to their safety. The word does not always have theological implications; one man may save another from peril, one army may save another from defeat. Nor does it always have negative overtones; it does not always mean "deliverance *from*." It can have a positive sense and refer to a bestowing on, a giving to. It can include all that a man may wish—all that one may expect in this life from a benevolent God, whose generous will is unopposed.

Salvation is both: security *from* and enjoyment *of*. It is first of all security—security from the sword, from pestilence, from famine; but it is also blessing, the blessing of the womb, of the field, of the barn; and it is life and length of days. It is these earthly and homely blessings, for, as we have noted, the age had not yet come when Jews thought in terms of heavenly reward.

For the Second Isaiah, salvation meant something more. His spirit was expansive, his horizon broad. His God was the one, unique world-God, universal in time as well as in space. To such a prophet, representing such a God, salvation must be something more, something commensurate with his spirit. According to this prophet salvation is world-wide. It is the goal God has set for mankind, the realization of the divine purpose in human society.

Out of chaos God created the world. Creation is purposive, and it is not to be reversed—creation should not revert to the *tohu va bohu* which it was before God spoke.

> Not to be an empty waste did He create it
> [the prophet said];
> to be inhabited He formed it (45:18).

Once because of human depravity He had been constrained to destroy with a cosmic flood all flesh and start anew with the family of Noah. Again, for men's arrogance, He had found it necessary to divide mankind into a Babel of unrecognizable tongues and scatter them over the earth. But both events were a slipping back, and what ground was lost was yet to be regained. Mankind divided into warring tribes, hopelessly unable to reach an understanding because their words have lost all meaning and so communication is cut off—such a society was not the goal of God's desires for humanity. Eventually the family of man must again be united. Their reunion is the goal; a reconciled humanity, this is salvation.

And it is the same as the messianic hope, the Utopian ideal which we have considered, God's kingdom on earth: when swords will be beaten into plowshares and spears into pruning hooks, when people will not raise sword against people or learn war any more, when each man may sit under his vine and his fig tree with none to make him afraid.

It is the hope that the lion will lie down with the lamb, that men in power will abandon their rapacious, predatory drives, and learn to live with the weak and the humble in active harmony. It is the hope for that beckoning time when men will "not hurt or destroy" in all God's holy mountain—in all this world which He made.

Now one may want to ask where we have got to and where we are going. We seem to have returned to themes which we have already considered, themes which we classed with the kind of faith that only accepts. And here we are, citing those shapes of hope that belong to that sort of faith, when we claim to be speaking of the products of the other kind of faith—the kind that requires doing.

THE MISSION OF THE SERVANT

But we have not wandered from the subject. The goal is the same for faith of both sorts; it is only a question of man's role in achieving the goal, whether he simply accepts or whether he has a job to do. According to the Second Isaiah he has a job to do. Or must we be more precise and say: "*Israel* has a job to do"? If we are speaking of the Second Isaiah this is what we should say; he assigned to *his people* a task, a role in the process of deliverance. That is the meaning of the figure known as "the servant of the Lord." It has broadened since his time, but when the Second Isaiah spoke of the servant of the Lord he spoke of Israel.

Consider this conception: "the servant of the Lord." Not every scholar will agree on the meaning of the servant. Not every Jew will agree. There is no single Jewish interpretation, nor any single Christian interpretation, either. Many will agree with the interpretation offered here (for the reasoning behind it, see Blank, *Prophetic Faith in Isaiah*, pp. 77-104), but it still is *an* interpretation, not *the* interpretation.

In the passages which interest us here, in all of them, even in the famous fifty-third which describes the "passion" of the servant, the servant is a personification of the people Israel. The servant was not understood in this way when the New Testament was written. To the authors of the New Testament the servant was not a people but a person, he was the hoped-for messiah. And to the extent th t the life and fate of Jesus followed the pattern of the servant, Jesus was identified as this messianic servant of the Lord. The Jewish interpretation of the Isaiah material current at the time of Jesus no doubt facilitated this identification. Jewish thinking had been moving in that direction. But the prophetic author of the sixteen chapters had no such meaning in mind.

Wherever we look in Isaiah 40 to 55 the servant is the people of Israel, chosen by God to serve Him, commissioned by God to bring witness. Let us reread a few passages quoted from there and decide for ourselves who the servant must be, setting aside while we read, if we can, any interpretation we are familiar with, in the New Testament, or in Jewish tradition, or elsewhere, and simply listening and judging for ourselves who the servant is. In the following three passages God is speaking. To whom is he speaking?

You, Israel My servant,
    Jacob whom I chose,
    seed of Abraham, My friend,
You whom I took from the ends of the earth,
    summoned from its distant parts
Saying to you: "You are My servant,"
    I favor you and I have not rejected you.
Do not fear for I am with you. . . . (41:8–10a).

Now hearken Jacob My servant,
    Israel whom I have chosen.
Thus says God your maker,
    He who formed you at birth, who will help you:
"Fear not, My servant Jacob,
    Jeshurun whom I have chosen" (44:1f.).

Remember these things, O Jacob,
    O Israel, for you are My servant.
I formed you; you are a servant to Me.
    O Israel, I will not forget you (44:21).

In another passage God speaks to the conquering Cyrus, His
agent, about His chosen servant:

For the sake of My servant Jacob,
    Israel My chosen one,
I summoned you by name,
    naming you though you know Me not (45:4).

It would be less than honest to say that there are no problems
at all, but certainly these and about a dozen other passages
make a fairly uniform impression; the servant of the Lord is
Jacob, Jeshurun, the chosen one, Israel—personified.

Personification is a literary device, a figure of speech. The
Second Isaiah was a master at personification. He could
develop a figure until his figment lives and we seem to have a
real person before us. And it is perhaps no wonder that later
times had trouble with his servant figure. He made it so life-
like that it could easily seem that he had a known person in
mind. If he had been less skillful the many volumes written

about the identity of the servant would not have been written. Everyone would have known: he meant Israel.

Now we could properly devote several chapters to this servant figure and even then have barely touched the subject. But in order to preserve reasonable proportions we will limit ourselves here to three observations. The first is brief, the others longer.

The first focuses on the word "servant." The Second Isaiah thinks of Israel as a servant. A servant serves, has a task, a job to do. If we seem to be repeating this thought, saying the same thing again and again though in different words, that is done in order to make the point. In personifying Israel as the servant of the Lord, the Second Isaiah assigned to his people not a passive but an active role, asked of his people the faith that requires doing. The very word he used, *'eved*, "servant," implies as much. It distinguishes the thought of the Second Isaiah from the thought of those authors of the messianic or apocalyptic passages which we have already reviewed. He goes along with those authors some of the way but then he parts with them. His goal is the same as that of the messianists, as we shall yet see, but attaining the goal will not be God's work alone; man has a role to play, a role in the redemptive process—a mission.

THE "SUFFERING" SERVANT?

What is this role? It is not martyrdom; that is the second observation and it can not be stated as briefly as the first. When they speak of "the servant" in these chapters Jews are inclined to toss in an adjective and to say, without even thinking: "the *suffering* servant." And Jews are not alone in this misconception. At first glance the description of the servant in Isaiah 52:13–53:12 gives reason enough for this view:

> . . . His looks were inhumanly marred,
>   his appearance unlike a man's (52:14).

> He was despised and ignored by men,
>   a man of pains, familiar with sickness,
> One to look away from . . . (53:3).

> He was driven and was meek,
>   not opening his mouth—
> As a sheep led to the slaughter,
>   as a ewe is dumb before her shearers—
>   not opening his mouth (53:7).

There is quite enough in this chapter to account for the image of Israel the suffering servant.

Nevertheless it is a false and a profitless image. It is false because the chapter speaks not of a people destined to suffer but of a people which has suffered. In the tense lies the error and the misconstruction. All the verbs in the verses just quoted are in the past tense. "His looks were . . . marred." "He was despised." "He was driven." That Israel had suffered was, of course, undeniable. Defeat, destruction, captivity had been its lot—were still its lot. There had even been meaning in their past suffering. The kings of the nations knew well what it meant. "Suffering which could lead to our welfare," they called it.

> Indeed, he has borne sickness for us. . . .
> He was [in fact] wounded because of our
>   transgressions,
>   crushed because of our iniquities.
> He experienced the suffering which might
>   lead to our welfare,
>   and there was healing for us in his bruises
>   (53:4a, 5).

This is a somewhat unusual and difficult thought but it is not unique in the Bible. Perhaps the most graphic parallel is one in Exodus, in 14:30f. Israel had just crossed the Red Sea. "So

God delivered Israel from Egypt on that day," we read. And then the suffering which might lead to this people's welfare: "And Israel saw Egypt dead on the shore of the sea. And Israel [thus] experienced God's great might, employed against Egypt, and the people both feared God and believed in God and His servant Moses." From what Egypt had suffered Israel learned and might derive profit. So from Israel's experience others might learn and profit.

According to the Second Isaiah there had been that much meaning in Israel's pain—there *had* been—in the past. Here the prophet stopped. He did not go on to say that for such a purpose Israel was yet to suffer, through future untold ages. He did not think of grief as Israel's destiny; he made of it neither a project nor a program. Quite the contrary! He spoke consistently of the suffering as over and past; a servant who had suffered, yes; a servant destined to suffer, no; the future is only radiant. Speaking for God, the prophet has this to say of Israel's future:

Lo, My servant shall prosper,
   shall rise, be lifted up, be greatly exalted (52:13)
[That is the prophet's expectation].

Even as many were appalled at him
   because his looks were inhumanly marred
   and his appearance unlike a man's (52:14)
[That is the misery and disgrace of the past, but it is followed by what shall yet be, namely:]

Even so many will be aghast at him;
   kings will be dumbfounded,
Having seen what had never been told them,
   having considered what they never had heard (52:15)
[That is to say, unheard-of glory is in store for the servant of God, for Israel—such future glory that the kings of nations shall be aghast].

The key words for the understanding of this chapter, the words revealing the prophet's original intent, are words

which he himself speaks of the servant in a climactic position
in the fifty-third chapter (vs. 10): "God's desire shall succeed
through him." This is an exciting thought about which we
shall want to say more.

This has been our observation about the idea of the "suffering" servant: that the Second Isaiah never meant to assign to
Israel, the servant of God, the role of a scapegoat, a vicarious
sacrifice. He never suggested martyrdom as his people's
future lot. We do not find in the servant image the idea of a
people by nature defeated before it begins.

A PEOPLE OF PROPHETS

What, then, is the role of the servant Israel according to the
Second Isaiah? The servant has the role of a prophet; and this
is the third observation, and it is not to be misunderstood. It
does not mean that the servant is any one prophet, known or
unidentified, past, present or future—the servant is, as we
have been saying, the people Israel, drawn in personification
to look like a prophet, with the features of a prophet—a
people sent to serve as a prophet must serve, and to accomplish what, ideally, a prophet may accomplish, sent to save
from ruin not a people (Israel) but mankind, sent to realize
God's wider purpose. "God's desire shall succeed through
him"—"through him"—that is what the Second Isaiah says of
the servant: "God's desire shall succeed through him"; and
this also is contained in that fifty-third chapter. Elsewhere too
the Second Isaiah represents God as saying:

> Here is My servant whom I uphold,
>   My chosen one in whom I delight.
> I have put My spirit on him;
>   he will publish truth among the nations (42:1).

That is his activity: publishing the truth.

God could say most of that about any of His other

prophets: I have put My spirit on him; he will publish the truth. The difference is in the last phrase: "among the nations." God put His spirit on single prophets and sent them to publish the truth among His people Israel. He sent His servant Israel, a whole prophet-people, according to the Second Isaiah—He sent this servant to publish the truth among the nations.

> He will not fade nor be broken [the passage continues],
>   until he establishes truth on earth.
> The coastlands wait for his teaching (42:4).

And in a similar passage God says:

> So I make you a light to the nations,
>   that My salvation may reach
>   to the ends
> of the earth (49:6b).

These are the words that draw it all together—Israel, the job, salvation, all that we have been talking about in this chapter—all in the words here spoken to Israel, the "servant": "I make you a light to the nations, that My salvation may reach to the ends of the earth."

Let the name Israel stand for all men who have a sense of dedication, commitment. Think of salvation as a state of blessedness and security *here*. Then listen again: "I make you a light to the nations, that My salvation may reach to the ends of the earth."

Combine a faith that requires doing with an orientation towards life here, and the result is: human efforts to improve the human state, the service brought by persons dedicated to the achievement of the messianic goal, that every man may enjoy freedom from fear and from want, and enjoy that freedom here.

And Who Is Jonah?

WHEN WE TURN FROM THE SECOND ISAIAH TO THE BOOK OF Jonah we are really not changing the subject—not if we understand Jonah. The Book of Jonah is simply an illustration of the servant theme.

Jonah is also among the prophets, one of the greatest of the prophets called "minor." The book is short—shorter still if we omit a piece that somehow got added to the original story, the psalm in the second chapter (verses 2–10).

Things in the Book of Jonah are not what they seem. The book is a piece of fiction, fiction with a sacred purpose. Discover what the persons and places in the story stand for and its purpose becomes clear. Only God, in this story, is who He seems to be. Every other character and place stands for someone or for something else.

Read the story, here offered with the intrusive psalm left out, and consider the probable identity of the characters and places. When the writer says "Jonah" whom does he mean? What does Nineveh represent if it is not here the capital of ancient Assyria? What is Tarshish if it is not to be understood as a distant Mediterranean port; and the ship and the storm and the fish, what are they if they are not simply a ship, a storm at sea and a whale? And what is the whole book about? Why did its author write it, and why may we associate it with the Second Isaiah's "servant of God"?

129

THE STORY

This is the story. The translation is new but, except for the one omission, quite close to the original:

> And the Lord said to Jonah the son of Amittai: Arise and go to that great city Nineveh and there announce its impending destruction. Jonah arose—but only to run off to Tarshish, contrary to God's directions. He went down to Joppa, found a vessel bound for Tarshish, paid the fare and went below, to go along to Tarshish, contrary to God's directions.
>
> But God hurled a gale wind at the sea and such a storm arose that the vessel was all but broken, and the awe-struck sailors loudly prayed each to his own god and hurled the cargo overboard to lighten the vessel.
>
> Meanwhile, within the belly of the ship Jonah lay asleep, until the captain came to him and said: What is this, you sleeper? Get up and pray to your god; perhaps he will take some note of us before we founder.
>
> Then they all consulted and agreed: We will cast lots to discover whose offense brought on us this calamity. They did so, and Jonah was taken.
>
> Whereupon they demanded: Tell us, author of our calamity, what you do, where you come from, what land, what people. And he replied: I am a Hebrew and I worship the Lord, the God of all the world, who made the sea as well as the dry land.
>
> Then the men were terrified and asked: "What then have you done?" though they knew, because he had told them, that he was

running away from God. As the seas raged more and more they asked: What can we do to still the waves? And he said: You must hurl me into the sea; only then will it be calm. I know that I have brought on this storm.

Nevertheless, the sailors rowed hard to gain the shore but could not, as the seas raged more and more. So they called on the Lord and said: "Ah, Lord! Let us not perish for the life of this man, and do not hold us guilty of shedding innocent blood. You, Lord, have done as You wished. After which words they lifted Jonah and hurled him into the sea. Immediately the sea stopped raging, and in earnest the men feared the Lord, offered Him sacrifices, and vowed vows.

As for Jonah, the Lord had a great fish ready to swallow him; and for three days and nights Jonah was in the belly of the fish. Then the Lord spoke, and the fish cast Jonah out onto the dry land.

Now for a second time, the Lord said to Jonah: Arise and go to that great city Nineveh, and there announce what I tell you. This time Jonah went, as the Lord said, to Nineveh.

Nineveh was a very great city, three days across, and Jonah having gone one day's distance, announced: Yet forty days and Nineveh will be destroyed!

But the people of Nineveh believed the Lord, and they proclaimed a fast and they all dressed in sackcloth, great and small. Word also reached the king of Nineveh, and he left his throne, changed from garments of state into sackcloth, sat among ashes, and issued this royal edict in Nineveh: Neither man nor beast, herd nor flock shall taste anything;

they shall not feed or drink water; but they shall put on sackcloth—man and beast—and pray mightily to God; and everyone shall turn from his evil way and cleanse his hands of violence. Who knows but that God may change and relent and leave off His anger, and we not perish?

Now God saw what they did, how they turned from their evil way, and God thought better of the harm that He had intended to do them and He did not do it.

Then Jonah was greatly displeased and angry. And he prayed: Ah, Lord! Did I not say so when I was still at home? That was why I faced about and ran for Tarshish, knowing that You are gracious, loving, patient, abundantly merciful and forgiving. Now, Lord, take away my life; it is better I should die than live. Then God said: Are you very angry?

And Jonah went from the city and sat to the east of it and made him a shelter there and waited in its shade to see what would happen in the city. The Lord also provided a gourd which grew up over Jonah to shade his head and save him from harm and Jonah took great pleasure in the gourd. But when the following day dawned the Lord provided a worm as well and it smote the gourd, and it wilted. Then when the sun came up the Lord brought on a sultry east wind and the sun beat down on the head of Jonah, and he felt faint and asked that he might die saying: It is better that I should die than live. Again God said to Jonah: Are you very angry because of the gourd? And he said: Angry to the point of death. And the Lord said: So you have pity on the gourd for which you did not toil, which you did not produce, which appeared in one night and vanished in one night. Surely then you will expect Me to have pity on that teeming city Nineveh with its population of over 120,000 simple persons, to say nothing of all the cattle.

THE QUESTIONS

That is the story. Now for the questions.

Who is Jonah?

His name appears twice in the Bible, once here in this book, and once briefly in the Book of Kings. In Kings he is mentioned quite incidentally as a prophet who lived at the time of Amos and the king Jeroboam II. According to that very brief notice in II Kings 14:25 this prophet Jonah ben Amittai foretold great victories for the armies of his king. *That* Jonah, about whom nothing whatever else is said or known, was a historical personality—not at all significant but historical. The other Jonah, the Jonah ben Amittai of the Book of Jonah, is not historical at all but *he* is very significant. He never lived; he is one of the really important characters in the Bible but he is a fiction, a metaphor. Historical and significant are not the same thing, as in an earlier context we observed.

It is important, this thought that historical and significant are not the same thing. Understand this thought and we read the Bible with a fresh appreciation. The *idea* of Sinai is meaningful far beyond the *event*. The Exodus is occasion enough for celebrating the ideal of freedom, as Jews do year by year, whether it is history or tradition. The command "A stranger shall you not oppress; for you know the heart of a stranger, seeing you were strangers in the land of Egypt" (Exod. 23:9) has a greatness that is wholly independent of the historicity of the Egyptian sojourn.

But let us stay with Jonah. The Book of Jonah is a

metaphor, a comparison, and Jonah is, like the servant, a kind of personification. He is Israel through the eyes of the author of the Book of Jonah. And the author of the Book of Jonah saw his people in that light because he was a spiritual descendant of the Second Isaiah and he was not pleased with his people's apparent failure to carry through its destined task. He invented the character of Jonah to serve as a characterization, or perhaps as a caricature, of Israel, a prophet people, assigned a prophetic role and loafing on the job. Jonah is any man, he is "everyman," a personification of any favored people that weakly drags its feet. When we are vulnerable Jonah is a caricature of us.

And what is the city of Nineveh? It is not the cruel seat of the ruthless Assyrian Empire—the capital city of Sargon and Shalmaneser—the Shalmaneser who attacked, the Sargon who defeated and deported the ten northern tribes, the capital of Assyria an ancient enemy. The author of Jonah was a preacher, and for this preacher's purpose in this story Nineveh is simply a foreign place, a remote place, neither friendly nor hostile, a place of men, wherever men are in trouble or need. Nineveh is the hungry world.

And what is the time of the story? We would guess that the book itself was written in the fifth pre-Christian century, some time after the Second Isaiah, but the time of the story is neither the fifth nor the eighth century—neither the author's time nor the time of the historical Jonah; it is the once-upon-a-time time, any time, our time.

And where is Tarshish? *What* is Tarshish? Tarshish is not a western Mediterranean port famous for its commerce and significant for itself; in the story it is anywhere—anywhere but the right place; it is the opposite direction, the direction a man takes when he turns his back on his destiny; it is the direction a political party takes, or a religious group or a nation, when it turns its back on its destiny, refuses to take on its mission. It is the excuses we give—our rationalizations.

And what is the great fish? The great fish is no whale, no known or unidentified, extinct or mythological monster of the sea. It is whatever prevents a man from running quite away—character, history, "fate" to the Greeks, to us, God—a manifestation of God's generous will.

So much for identities. Now how do the persons behave in the story? What are they like?

Jonah is a Jew; he says so: "I am a Hebrew and I worship the Lord, the God of all the world, who made the sea as well as the dry land." He is also by definition a prophet, one to whom God has said "Go." "Arise and go to that great city Nineveh and there announce its impending destruction." He is also the "hero" of the story but in his behavior he is neither Jew nor prophet and he is more lethargic than heroic. Quite as striking as the words the author puts in the mouth of Jonah ("It is better that I should die than live") are the symbols he uses: the hold of the ship and the belly of the fish. They are symbols, and they mean refuge from the responsibilities of living. It was no punishment for Jonah to sojourn in the fish. That is a misunderstanding. The belly of the fish was snug and secure, a place where again he could sleep as he had slept before deep in the hold of the ship, oblivious of the roaring storm, with no need to do anything. Jonah is the type of man or the kind of a people that values "peace of mind" above life's demands. He is satisfied to drowse in the comfortable fish. And living, he is just half alive—a spectator only. He makes him a shelter to the east of Nineveh and waits there in its shade to see what will happen in the city.

The author has a more positive attitude towards the other persons in his story—the Gentiles, the people of the other nations. To be sure he calls them "simple persons"; in the Hebrew idiom the people of Nineveh "do not know their right hand from their left." He thinks of them as simple, unlearned, religiously naïve, probably so because God had not given them the Torah; it was Jonah's people who were the privileged custodians of the ancient wisdom. And these other men worship other gods. When the storm raged, "the awestruck sailors loudly prayed each to his own god."

But a most remarkable feature of the book is the fact that its author regards these naïve sailors and these same simple Ninevites as both good and generous, sensitive and open-minded. To be sure the Ninevites had done wrong; it was to condemn them and to announce their punishment that Jonah came (unwillingly) to them. But they listened to him. Bitterly and repeatedly, prophets whom God sent to the Jews (Amos, Micah, Isaiah, Jeremiah, Ezekiel, even the Second Isaiah) complained that their insensitive people Israel did *not* listen, could not hear them. Perhaps those frustrated prophets were harder on their people than their people's behavior warranted, but they did insist that this stiff-necked people persistently refused to listen (see Ezek. 3:6f.). But—the king and people of Nineveh listened. Not only did they not mock the prophet but in a dynamic sense they listened: they believed the word and prayed mightily and turned everyone from his evil way and cleansed their hands of violence. They repented and did right.

The sailors, too, the assorted crew of sailors on the vessel bound for Tarshish, were both reasonable and generous. They tried to spare Jonah. After they had done all they could do according to their light, after they themselves had prayed aloud, jettisoned the cargo, awakened Jonah to pray as well, cast lots and found whose offense had aroused the calamitous storm, even after Jonah had told them how they could calm the waves, even then they showed their generous nature. They did not do as he had said until they had exhausted their strength pulling at the oars to save him if they could.

And when the miracle had happened and suddenly the waves were still, "they feared the Lord." Like Darius and Nebuchadnezzar in the Book of Daniel, like Jethro and Naaman, and Pharaoh even, impressed by the miracle, the sailors "feared the Lord, offered Him sacrifices and vowed vows." To the healthy-minded author of the Book of Jonah the nations were both reasonable and worthy—and Jonah's service for their sake was neither unrewarding nor a waste.

Now, two more questions. The one: Why in the first place was Nineveh doomed to destruction? It was not because the king and people had failed to perform the proper rituals to their gods, not that they had brought no sacrifices or wrong sacrifices, neglected hallowed rites and ceremonies, not because they were "not religious." Also it was not because Nineveh had offended against the people of Israel. It might well have been this latter. If the Jonah of our story had been the historical Jonah and had lived to see Assyria conquer Samaria and cruelly disperse its populace, that affront might well have been considered the cause for the impending destruction—Nineveh doomed in retaliation, Israel's God avenging His people's hurt.

But neither of these reasons, neither want of "religion" nor national resentment figures in the present story. The people of Nineveh are condemned only because of crimes committed within her walls, crimes against persons, offenses against what is just and right. And as soon as the people listened to Jonah and turned from those evil ways God readily forgave them. That was all it took, and pity moved the prophetic author of Jonah, not resentment—a moral sense, not national indignation.

The final question is about God. What is the nature of God in Jonah? The God of Jonah is not limited, not fenced in by territorial boundaries. He had fashioned the far-off city of Nineveh and He cared what went on there. The victims of injustice in that alien land were His clients quite as naturally as were the Hebrew slaves in Jerusalem in the days of Jeremiah. The distant port of Tarshish was not beyond His reach. He had made and still ruled the sea as well as the dry land. It is because his God knows no territorial limits that Jonah is sent to Nineveh, and it is because his God is the

Lord of all, that Jonah cannot escape his mission even by way of the sea. Jonah's God is beyond geography.

THE MEANING OF JONAH

The Book of Jonah is an illustrated sermon—one of the greatest sermons ever preached—and this is what the preacher meant to say: that any man who sees himself in Jonah is sent like Jonah to the Ninevehs of this earth, given a mission to the needy, a job to do. That is what the author meant; we do not read this meaning into the book, we find it there. And also this he meant to say: that the most of us, like Jonah, laggard, disinclined, avoid our mission, sail away if we can to some imagined Tarshish, watch from a shelter, slumber in the cabin.

With this we close. The prophets have supplied the text; the Book of Jonah is the illustration. All that is programmatic in the prophets, all the doing that their faith requires of us, all that the servant-prophet-people theme implies, is summed up in this little book. It comes very close to us. Jonah steps on our toes.